ROUTLEDGE LIBRARY EDITIONS:
THE ECONOMICS AND BUSINESS OF
TECHNOLOGY

Volume 25

THE RISE, DECLINE, AND RENEWAL OF SILICON VALLEY'S HIGH TECHNOLOGY INDUSTRY

THE RISE, DECLINE, AND RENEWAL OF SILICON VALLEY'S HIGH TECHNOLOGY INDUSTRY

DAN M. KHANNA

Routledge
Taylor & Francis Group

LONDON AND NEW YORK

First published in 1997 by Garland Publishing Inc.

This edition first published in 2018
by Routledge
2 Park Square, Milton Park, Abingdon, Oxon OX14 4RN

and by Routledge
711 Third Avenue, New York, NY 10017

Routledge is an imprint of the Taylor & Francis Group, an informa business

© 1997 Dan M. Khanna

British Library Cataloguing in Publication Data
A catalogue record for this book is available from the British Library

ISBN: 978-1-138-50336-6 (Set)
ISBN: 978-1-351-06690-7 (Set) (ebk)
ISBN: 978-0-8153-5289-1 (Volume 25) (hbk)
ISBN: 978-0-8153-5361-4 (Volume 25) (pbk)
ISBN: 978-1-351-13590-0 (Volume 25) (ebk)

Publisher's Note
The publisher has gone to great lengths to ensure the quality of this reprint but points out that some imperfections in the original copies may be apparent.

Disclaimer
The publisher has made every effort to trace copyright holders and would welcome correspondence from those they have been unable to trace.

THE RISE, DECLINE, AND RENEWAL OF SILICON VALLEY'S HIGH TECHNOLOGY INDUSTRY

DAN M. KHANNA

GARLAND PUBLISHING, Inc.
New York & London / 1997

Library of Congress Cataloging-in-Publication Data

Khanna, Dan M., 1946–
    The rise, decline, and renewal of Silicon Valley's high tech-
nology industry / Dan M. Khanna.
        p.   cm. — (Garland studies on industrial productivity)
    Includes bibliographical references and index.
    ISBN 0-8153-2724-2 (alk. paper)
    1. Microelectronics industry—California—Santa Clara
County. 2. High technology industries—California—Santa Clara
County. 3. Microelectronics industry—California—Santa Clara
County—Management. 4. Competition, International. I. Title.
II. Series.
HD9696.A3U5629 1997
338.4'7621381'0979473—dc21

                                                            96-49746

Printed on acid-free, 250-year-life paper
Manufactured in the United States of America

To my parents

To my parents

Contents

Illustrations

Figures

Tables

Tables

Preface

Why do some regions in the world emanate to transform the direction of our society and our way of living? Italy, during the Renaissance period, was such a region that shaped our thoughts, ideas, and its culture. During the last thirty years, Silicon Valley has significantly contributed to transform our society from the industrial age to the information age. Not only has it achieved global prominence, but its success is emulated around many regions of the world.

I was privileged to be a part of this exciting region during its emergence as the greatest electronics and technology center of the world. I observed the rise and fall of Fairchild Semiconductor, the father of all the semiconductor companies, a company that does not exist anymore. I noted the failure of Xerox Research Park to capitalize on its many inventions. I noticed the growth of Intel, Rolm Corporation, National Semiconductor, Advanced Micro Devices, Cypress Semiconductor, and many other companies that came, contributed, and disappeared. I experienced the emergence of Apple Computers, Silicon Graphics, and Sun Microsystems, all companies that helped shape the computer industry. As new industries and firms evolved through this technology revolution, firms like 3Com and Bay Networks shaped our electronic network communication perceptions. Software firms like Oracle and Sybase created database management systems. Numerous innovative software firms like Adobe and Macromedia ushered in a new era of multimedia and graphics technology. Netscape and Yahoo changed our thinking about the Internet and its communication advantages. This revolution still persists as Silicon Valley continues to dominate and shape the technology revolution worldwide.

But not all this transformation has been without its pain and problems. The region went through a few recessions during the 1980s. It lost competitiveness and substantial market share to international firms old and new. The growth created a high-cost of living that became unaffordable for many. Many jobs were lost. Traffic became a gridlock as the public sector was unable to properly plan for its growth. Much of the manufacturing growth of the 1970s slowed or vanished during the 1980s. As an active participant in this adventure, I enjoyed and sometimes felt the pain of the roller coaster life of this valley.

These observations led to the research for this book. I was curious to understand the unique nature and characteristics of this region. I wanted to learn the factors that led to the meteoric rise of the Silicon Valley. I also wanted to understand the factors that led to the serious economic and competitiveness problems of the 1980s. Since the unique entrepreneurial management and technology innovation have consistently been integral characteristics of the Silicon Valley, I was curious to learn what other factors may have caused its problems during the 1980s. My research led me to conclude that this information revolution caused a complex set of events that led to global ramifications. Silicon Valley was no longer operating as a driver of this revolution, but it was also facing the onslaught of the global competitiveness that it had unleashed.

For Silicon Valley to maintain its domination and success in the next century, it will need to understand and learn from its history of the last thirty years. This book attempts to provide some of the answers.

This study is a personal journal. As I was working in the Valley, I was able to observe the changes and some of the causes. I had the opportunity to talk to many of my colleagues in the business and industry. An excellent network of information exists in the Valley, and I was able to tap on to some of those sources. Numerous articles in newspapers and magazines frequently discuss the issues and challenges of the Valley. They provided valuable knowledge and information.

I thank many people: friends, colleagues, students, peers, academic advisers, and business leaders who have provided valuable insight into the workings of Silicon Valley. Mostly I thank my family for being supportive in my work and enduring my unconventional approach to life.

Dan Khanna

The Rise, Decline, and Renewal of Silicon Valley's High Technology Industry

Chapter 1

The Silicon Valley Revolution

> America is a land of wonders, in which
> everything is in constant motion and every
> change seems an improvement. . . . no
> natural boundary seems to be set to the
> efforts of man; and in his eyes, what is not
> yet done is only what he has not yet
> attempted to do.

> *Alexis de Tocqueville*
> Democracy in America

THE ADVENT OF THE INFORMATION AGE

Silicon Valley is the birthplace of the microelectronics
technology revolution that created semiconductors, microprocessors,
and personal computers. These discoveries ushered in a new era of
information processing and communications systems that altered the
world's economic, business, and industrial structures and gave rise to
interdependent global markets. In its relatively short history of thirty
years, Silicon Valley transported our society from the industrial age to
the information age.[1] Unprecedented technology, especially the
application of microprocessors and the confluence of computers and
communications, made this change possible. The impact of this
technology transgresses existing boundaries of businesses and
industries refashioning them into political and economic structures.
Harlan Cleveland, an eminent political scientist, commented:

> The information revolution has stormed the
> ramparts of the nation-state, and most of
> our favorite economic theories, capitalist as
> well as Marxist, have been trampled in the
> rush.[2]

The emergence of global interdependent economies is also attributed
to this technology revolution, according to Harlan Cleveland.

> What made world business an
> increasingly single market was not
> primarily trade, aid, or alliances . . . what
> happened was that with the help offast
> computers and reliable telecommunications,
> capital (because it is a form of information)
> could flow so much faster and more freely
> than things.[3]

The impact of microelectronics impinges upon nearly every
industry and human endeavor. In his book, *The New Alchemists*, Dirk
Hanson describes some typical scenarios:

> Microelectronics has become an
> indispensable part of the practice of modern
> science. . . . in complex diagnostic and
> critical care equipment. Communications
> systems for the speechless and seeing-eye
> microcomputer systems for the blind . . . In
> the burgeoning field of
> telecommunications, the microchips forging
> a link between the telephone, the computer
> and the television.
>   The arts are not immune: electronic
> music and composition are commonplace,
> while visual artists explore, and sometimes
> fret over, computer-generated graphics and
> electronic three-dimensional sketch pads.
>   Nor is education: microcomputers are
> common classroom teaching tools. Scholars
> pouring over ancient manuscripts routinely

make use of computer systems for
deciphering.[4]

This microcomputer revolution is fundamentally different from
other technological revolutions. "It promises tochange not only the
way we live, but ultimately the way we think,"[5] according to Joseph
Deken, author of *The Electronic Cottage.*

The way businesses are conducted and managed has been
permanently modified. As Derek Leebaert stated in *Technology 2001*
"Information technologies are now the strategic core of business."[6]
According to Don Tapscott and Art Caston, authors of *Paradigm
Shift: The New Promise of Information Technology*:

> We are entering a second era of information
> technology in which the business
> applications of computers, the nature of the
> technology itself, and the leadership for use
> of technology are all going through
> profound change.[7]

The impact of the information technology paradigm shift on
businesses is explained by Tapscott and Caston:

> Businesses face a paradox. They have
> unprecedented opportunities to tap new
> markets. Meanwhile, traditional markets
> are changing dramatically, shrinking or
> becoming intensely competitive.
> Additionally, reduced profit margins along
> with rising customer demands for quality
> products and services are placing
> unrelenting pressures on many enterprises.[8]

The endowment of Silicon Valley to this paradigm shift is expounded
by Hanson:

> As the nerve center of the microelectronics
> revolution for the past twenty-five years,
> Silicon Valley has gained a well-deserved
> reputation as the Florence of the

> information age. It houses perhaps the
> densest concentration of high-technology
> brain power in the world; a heady mix of
> digital circuit and computer manufacturers,
> Nobel Prize winners, maverick scientists,
> university researchers, electronic warfare
> specialists and high-octane investors.[9]

As society continues to assimilate information technologies, the future contribution of Silicon Valley is still undetermined. Its role in the twenty-first century will be determined by its ability to learn from its successes and failures of the past thirty years.

THE PREMISE OF THE BOOK

The growth of Silicon Valley during the 1970s was characterized by its technological innovation, availability of capital, entrepreneurial spirit, and highly skilled work force. The same characteristics existed during the 1980s decline years, which leads to the conclusion that there were other external factors in the world economy that may have played a dominant part in the decline of Silicon Valley. Eventually, management is held responsible for the success and failure of the business enterprise. As the global economic competitiveness changed, Silicon Valley's management failed to respond to those changes. Furthermore, it lost competitiveness to regions in the world that had minimal economic infrastructures, limited knowledge of high-technology, and untrained work forces.

The decline is attributed to the shift in market and economic forces around the globe caused by the microelectronic revolution and the creation of comparativeadvantages by other regions and firms in other parts of the world, especially, Asia Pacific region.

The resurgence of Silicon Valley during the mid-1990s was the result of lessons learnt from some of its failures, the shift in the high-technology industry from hardware to software domination, and the creating of new industries and applications, such as multimedia, networking, and communications.

Is this resurgence a temporary aberration that could shift again to different regions as these new industries mature?

The objective of this study is:

- To analyze the reasons that caused the emergence of Silicon Valley,
- Examine the market, economic, and competitive forces that made possible Silicon Valley's growth,
- Determine the reasons for its declining competitiveness during the 1980s,
- Analyze its resurgence and renewal during the 1990s, and
- Recommend specific courses of action by which Silicon Valley firms can prevent and maintain their world leadership position.

The Argument

The theory of comparative advantage attempts to explain the international success in industries in the form of international trade according to Michael Porter.[10] Adam Smith is credited with the notion of absolute advantage, while David Ricardo refined this notion to that of comparative advantage, "recognizing that market forces will allocate a nation's resources to those industries where it is relatively more productive."[11]

However, contemporary scholars argue that globalization and technological changes may only provide "fleeting advantages" to an industry and the comparative advantage factors may rapidly change. The industry that is unable to respond to these changes will no longer remain competitive in the global economy.[12]

The major issues that the book examines and explains are:

1. What factors and comparative advantages led to the meteoric rise of the Silicon Valley electronics industry in such a short time? Did Silicon Valley possess unique advantages? What were those advantages? Did they cause the growth? Were these factors of chance or were they man-made? Can this be repeated, here or anywhere else?
2. What forces and factors caused the decline in the Silicon Valley's competitiveness and its loss of major world market share during the 1980s? Were these developments simply the result of world-wide competitive forces or were they attributed to the business strategies and management practices of Silicon Valley

firms? What comparative advantages existed overseas? Were they
created, and if so, how and why? Or, was the decline a natural
phenomena of the industry's life cycle?

3. What market, industry, and technology factors led to the
    resurgence of Silicon Valley during the 1990s for it to regain its
    world competitive position? Is it in a leadership position? Is this
    renewal permanent? Can Silicon Valley lose its competitiveness
    again?

4. What lessons can be learnt and implemented such that Silicon
    Valley does not lose its competitive position again? What
    comparative advantages does it need to create? What does it need
    to do? What adjustment it needs to make to maintain its dominant
    position in the next century?

The book's findings will be beneficial to the industry, to
Silicon Valley leaders, executives, and professionals, to government
officials in commerce and economics, and to other regions, domestic
and overseas, that are trying to emulate Silicon Valley.

ITS SIGNIFICANCE TO THE AMERICAN ECONOMY

The significance of Silicon Valley to the United States loss of
competitiveness cannot be overestimated. In addition to being a major
contributor to the nation's economy, it also exemplifies the industry
of the future. A *San Jose Mercury* article commented on the
contribution of Silicon Valley firms to the U.S. economy:

> The national economy has barely stirred
> from two years of hibernation, but business
> for Silicon Valley's largest companies has
> been perking along as though the recession
> never occurred. . . . sales for Silicon
> Valley's top companies increased more than
> 15 percent at a time when sales for the
> Fortune 500 inched upward 4 percent and

the national economy grew only 2.1 percent.[13]

Applications of the new electronic technologies have spread to all other major industries, including automobiles, agriculture, materials sciences, medical technology, biotechnology, and genetic engineering. Recent commentary in a *San Francisco Chronicle* article elaborated:

> Most Americans may not realize it, but they own scores of semiconductors even if they have never touched a personal computer. Computer chips are now embedded in everything from autos and alarm clocks to TVs and thermostats, microwave ovens and lawn mowers. The fingernail-size slices of silicon etched with millions of electronic circuits keep car brakes from locking up, let you program recordings of TV programs on your VCR—make all those smart products that help you control your life.[14]

Additionally, the nation's security rests on continuing technological advancement and competitiveness, as was evident in the recent Gulf War. It also became apparent in that war that the United States has become dependent on foreign firms for numerous key components for its weapon systems. Most major technological breakthroughs are still created in Silicon Valley, but are then arrogated by the rest of the world. As Daniel Burstein explained in his book *Turning the Tables:*

Although Americans continue to dominate the development of basic science and many kinds of basic technological research, there is no sign yet that the United States has reversed its long-standing difficulties in commercializing, manufacturing, and selling the fruits of its creative innovation.[15]

A report published by the U.S. Department of Commerce on "The Competitive Status of the U.S. Electronics Sector," identified six major reasons for the significance of the high-technology sector to the U.S. economy:[16]

1. It is the major growth sector in the U.S. economy.
2. It is "a major source of new firm creation and is composed of a high percentage of small firms."
3. It is a major source of attraction of foreign investment in the United States.
4. It is also a major source of innovation that could create new industries and markets.
5. It is also a major sector for export.
6. It is also a major source for innovation that could lead to advancements in productivity in other sectors.

Since Silicon Valley is still the largest electronic agglomeration in the world, its success and growth is vital to U.S. worldwide competitiveness. Frequent visits to Silicon Valley by President Clinton and Vice President Gore testify to the importance of this region. The federal government study has reiterated that Silicon Valley's revitalization and contribution is critical to the U.S. economic recovery and success.[17] It also proposed a "new partnership" between government and private business "to create thousands of new jobs in Silicon Valley over the next five years."[18] The Clinton administration is also supporting and endorsing a public and private consortium called Joint Venture: Silicon Valley "to kick-start Silicon Valley's sluggish economy,"[19] and to work towards maintaining its competitive advantage in the future by working with business, government, and education professionals.

Protracted loss of Silicon Valley's competitiveness would be a major blow to the future economic and industrial strength of the United States.

BOOK OVERVIEW

This study is a culmination of four years of research into the dynamics of Silicon Valley. Research for this book began in 1990 when various articles appeared in newspapers, magazines, and journals questioning the future of Silicon Valley. Articles continued to provide valuable information during the preparation of this book.

The current body of literature on Silicon Valley consists of articles in journals and magazines that has examined, evaluated, and critiqued different aspects of Silicon Valley; books written specifically on Silicon Valley; books that imply or comment on some aspects of Silicon Valley; statistical data from government and industrial publications; newspaper commentaries on events and issues relating to Silicon Valley; and statements by Silicon Valley executives, professionals, and experts. Besides the above published material, research data and information accumulated through personal business dealings and discussions with many Silicon Valley executives, authorities, and professionals were utilized. This book integrates that material.

The complexity of the study cuts across many disciplines and demonstrates the interdependence of economic, business, political, global, and ideological factors. To distinguish the appropriate reasons for the growth and decline of Silicon Valley, diverse subjects, such as macroeconomic principles, national ideologies, business orthodoxies, and management philosophies were reviewed, analyzed, and integrated. A relevant theoretical framework is provided to facilitate the elaboration of the study.

Chapter 1 explores the information age, explains the premise of the book, discusses the importance of Silicon Valley, and provides an overall perspective of the book. Chapter 2 presents the appropriate data and pertinent information on the growth and decline of Silicon Valley, its current situation, and the challenges it faces for the next century.

The relevant macroeconomic theory, principles, and national ideologies are discussed in Chapters 3, 4, and 5. A firm or an industry is an economic entity and global economic shifts affect its competitiveness. Chapter 3 explores the economic shift during the last thirty years and its impact on the competitiveness of American firms. Chapter 4 synthesizes the role of national and business ideologies on competitive forces and economic development policies. Chapter 5 expounds the theory of comparative advantage and its relevance to the Silicon Valley issue.

Chapter 6 describes the factors that caused the genesis and growth of Silicon Valley, propelling it toworld-wide prominence. It analyzes the unique characteristics and comparative advantages that enabled its success. [20]

The shift, and the causes of the shift, in comparative advantages from Silicon Valley to foreign firms and industries is discussed in Chapters 7 and 8. It explains the actions, interactions, and steps taken by Silicon Valley and foreign firms that facilitated the process. Chapter 7 focuses on the internal actions and dynamics of the Silicon Valley and Chapter 8 explains the external factors that caused the shift in comparative advantages.

The decline of Silicon Valley, from its own perspective and the perspective of different experts, is analyzed in Chapter 9.

Finally, Chapter 10 offers specific suggestions for Silicon Valley to reinvent itself and create new comparative advantages that would enable it to regain and retain global high-technology dominance into the twenty-first century.

NOTES

1. John Naisbitt, *Megatrends: Ten New Directions Transforming Our Lives* (New York: William Morrow and Company, 1982), 11.

2. Harlan Cleveland, *Birth of a New World* (San Francisco: Jossey-Bass Publishers, 1993), 139.

3. Ibid, 138.

4. Dirk Hanson, *The New Alchemists: Silicon Valley and the Micro-Electronics Revolution* (New York: Avon Books, 1982), 128.

5. Joseph Deken, *The Electronic Cottage* (New York: Bantam Books, 1981), 1.

6. Derek Leebaert, ed. Technology 2001: *The Future of Computing and Communications* (Cambridge: The MIT Press, 1990), 4.

7. Don Tapscott and Art Caston, *Paradigm Shift: The New Promise of Information Technology* (New York: McGraw Hill, 1993), 13.

8. Ibid., 4.

9. Hanson, *The New Alchemists*, xi.

10. Michael E. Porter, *The Competitive Advantage of Nations* (New York: The Free Press, 1990), 11.

11. Ibid., 11.

12. Ibid., 15.

13. *San Jose Mercury News*, 11 April 1993.

14. Ken Siegmann, "Computer Chips Take Center Stage in Daily Life," *San Francisco Chronicle*, 20 December 1993, B1 and B3.

15. Daniel Burstein, *Turning the Tables: A Machiavellian Strategy for Dealing with Japan* (New York: Simon and Schuster, 1993), 173.

16. U.S. Department of Commerce, "The Competitive Status of the U.S. Electronics Sector from Materials to Systems," (Washington D.C.: U.S. Government Printing Office, 1990), 1-10.

17. Michael Zielenziger and Steve Kaufman, "A Prescription for Silicon Valley's Trade Ills," *San Jose Mercury News*, 20 July 1993, 1E and 7E.

18. Ibid., E1.

19. Ibid., E1.

Chapter 2

Growth, Decline, and Renewal Examined

From its inception in the late sixties, Silicon Valley dominated the worldwide semiconductor and microprocessor markets. Through innovation of new manufacturing processes, it created products for applications in existing and new industries. Financed by eager venture capitalists seeking to profit from this emerging industry, semiconductor firms sprouted throughout the valley, producing and marketing their products for the domestic and international markets. The demand significantly exceeded the supply.

To meet the demands of the worldwide market it had created, Silicon Valley generated over 100,000 manufacturing jobs between 1972 and 1980, and "by the end of 1984, there were over 2,500 high-tech firms employing almost 300,000 people.[1] The explosive growth and dominance of the Silicon Valley semiconductor and microelectronic industry is explained by Dirk Hanson:

> In fact, the revolutionaries of Silicon Valley cannot be fully aware of what they are doing because they can never foresee all the ways in which each new generation of digital devices will be put to work by creative users. The first microprocessor was intended for use in a Japanese calculator, nothing more. By 1980 the industry had delivered more than ten million microprocessors, and a complete listing of all the ways in which they are used would fill a telephone book. This

15

explosion of applications was neither intended nor expected, but one aspect of the microelectronics revolution has been clear since the beginning: inventing new media of communication is a profitable business. Silicon Valley is the reason why the top fifty electronic firms racked up $88.4 billion in sales in 1978, or about four percent of that year's total GNP.[2]

According to the 1989 study conducted by The MIT Commission on Industrial Productivity:

The U.S. semiconductor industry dominated world markets . . . when the transistor was first commercialized, through most of the 1970s. In the mid-1970s, when the American industry was at the height of its success, it held 60 percent of the world market, 95 percent of the domestic market, and a half of the European market, but only a fourth of the Japanese market.[3]

As other regions and international firms began to imitate the success of Silicon Valley and compete with it in world markets, the monopolistic and innovative comparative advantage of Silicon Valley firms commenced to erode. The firms began to lose worldwide market share; and, during the eighties, they were losing even their technological competitiveness. According to Dataquest, a reputed market research firm located in Silicon Valley, by 1989, Silicon Valley firms controlled only 35% of the world semiconductor market and 57% of the data processing equipment market, markets they had dominated and monopolized just twenty years earlier.[4] Andrew Grove, founder of Intel, the corporation that developed the microprocessor, described the phenomena as "the Technological Tsunami." (Tsunami is the Japanese word for tidal wave.) Before the wave strikes, "the industry in this country is doing its job reasonably well, but after the wave crashes, whatever is left of the industry in this country is decimated, weakened, and a minority supplier, with the majority supplier being Japanese."

In 1970, the United States controlled over 90% of the world semiconductor market. In 1986, Japan overtook the United States in market share and continued to increase its market, controlling over 50% of the world market in 1988. Since then, American firms have recovered some market share, but no longer control the semiconductor industry. Table 2.1 illustrates the dramatic change since 1980 in the world market share between the United States and Japan. Considering that Japan had virtually no experience in the semiconductor industry in 1970, this is a remarkable achievement for that country.

TABLE 2.1

SEMICONDUCTORS: WORLDWIDE MARKET (1980-1993)
(U.S., Japan, and Others, Market Share Percent)

Year	U.S.	Japan	Other
1980	57%	33%	10%
1984	54%	37%	9%
1985	49%	41%	10%
1986	42%	46%	12%
1987	41%	48%	11%
1988	37%	51%	11%
1989	37%	50%	12%
1990	40%	47%	13%
1991	39%	46%	14%
1992	43%	43%	14%
1993	43%	42%	15%

Source: Dataquest.
         Semiconductor Industry Association.

Even though Silicon Valley firms initiated the semiconductor industry, it was unable to meet the worldwide demand, and American firms depended on foreign firms for their supply of semiconductors. Table 2.2 compares the import and exports of semiconductors for United States.

TABLE 2.2

SEMICONDUCTORS: IMPORTS AND EXPORTS (1989-1994)
(in billions of dollars)

Item	1989	1990	1991	1992	1993	1994
Imports	12.2	12.0	12.9	15.3	17.9	20.6
Exports	9.5	10.7	10.8	11.5	13.6	15.7

Source: Dataquest.
Semiconductor Industry Association.

The market change for data processing equipment, which includes computer and communications equipment, is even more dramatic, as illustrated in Table 2.3. Again, the United States dominated the world in 1980 with more than 80% of the market.

TABLE 2.3

DATA PROCESSING EQUIPMENT: WORLDWIDE MARKET
(1980-1992)
(U.S.-Owned Vs. Japan-Owned Companies)
(Market Share Percent)

	1980	1984	1988	1989	1992
U.S.	82%	79%	63%	57%	38%
Japan	10%	12%	25%	28%	42%

Source: U.S. Department of Commerce, SIA (1992).

Not only did the United States computer industry decline in worldwide market share, but relied on imports to meet the domestic demand, as shown in Table 2.4.

TABLE 2.4

COMPUTERS AND PERIPHERALS: IMPORTS AND EXPORTS
(1989-1994)
(in billions of dollars)

Item	1989	1990	1991	1992	1993	1994
Imports	21.7	23.3	26.4	32.1	40.2	46.2
Exports	22.4	24.1	25.2	26.3	27.1	29.2

Source: U.S. Department of Commerce, International Trade
Administration.

The dramatic decline in market share of various Silicon Valley
companies continued in multifarious segments of the electronics
industry. A U.S. Commerce Department report, published in April
1990, illustrated the results from 1984 to 1987, as shown in Table
2.5.

TABLE 2.5

DECLINE OF U.S. SHARE OF WORLDWIDE ELECTRONICS
MARKETS FROM 1984 TO 1987 (Percent)

	1984	1987
Silicon Wafers	85	22
DRAMs	20	8
Laptop computers	85	57
Supercomputers	96	77
Displays	11	8
Floppy Drives	35	2

Source: U.S. Department of Commerce.

In 1975, Silicon Valley firms like Fairchild Semiconductor, Intel Corporation, National Semiconductor, and Advanced Micro Devices dominated the markets. By 1989, the top four semiconductor firms were NEC, Toshiba, Hitachi, Fujitsu, all Japanese. Fairchild Semiconductor, which had founded the semiconductor revolution in the 1960s, did not exist.

Even though the "worldwide production has continued to grow, the United States is no longer leading the growth."[5] What the market share decline numbers do not indicate is the slippage of Silicon Valley firms in future technological competitiveness. According to the MIT Study:

> The erosion of the U.S. position is even worse than these figures suggest, because both the American decline and the Japanese progress are steepest in some of the most advanced and important semiconductor markets and technologies. Japanese firms now hold 40 percent of the world market for microprocessors, 65 percent for microcontrollers, and 40 percent for application-specific integrated circuits (ASICs), a high growth market. The slippage is also severe in research and development for future technology.[6]

This statement is further collaborated by George Lodge in his book *Perestroika for America*:

> There are many varieties of semiconductors, but dynamic random access memory (DRAM) chips set the pace for progress in semiconductor technology because their key components more readily permit feature reduction, which increases the chip's power more easily compared to complex logic chips. Between 1975 and 1988, the U.S. share of the world merchant DRAM business declined from nearly 100

percent to less than 8 percent, most having
been taken away by Japanese firms.[7]

Innovation for new products can also be measured by the
number of patents awarded to firms. In a study by the Commerce
Department, among the top ten firms that were awarded U.S. patents,
none were from Silicon Valley, and Canon, Hitachi, and Toshiba
from Japan were the top three firms accounting for 2515 patents
between them.

During the growth of Silicon Valley firms in the 1970s,
hundreds of thousand of jobs were created. During the decline in the
1980s, many jobs were lost and the local economy was battered. A
1993 article in the *San Francisco Chronicle* noted:

> Battered by California's lingering
> recession, defense industry cutbacks and
> brutal competition in the computer sector,
> Silicon Valley is not only hemorrhaging
> jobs but losing a cultural edge that attracted
> talent from around the world in the past
> decade. . . . Meanwhile, round after round
> of layoffs have hit Silicon Valley
> companies. So far this year [Summer
> 1993], more than 8,600 jobs have been
> lost, compared with 4,600 by this time last
> year.[8]

The decline in electronics jobs in California since 1989 is
shown in Table 2.6.

TABLE 2.6

CALIFORNIA ELECTRONICS EMPLOYMENT (1989-1993)
(in hundreds of thousands)

Item	1989	1990	1991	1992	1993
Total Employed	730	705	680	605	575
Jobs Lost	0	25	25	75	30

Source: Spectrum Economics.[9]

Not all job cutbacks were caused by the competitive decline. In order to remain in contention worldwide, Silicon Valley firms effectuated business strategies that also contributed to the decline of jobs. As stated in the above article: "Production workers have faced job insecurity since the late 1970s, as high-tech companies shifted manufacturing jobs to states and countries with lower wages and housing costs and fewer workplace regulations."[10]

Silicon Valley grew because it capitalized on new technological inventions which created a new industry and also sustained a monopolistic control on manufacturing and market distribution during the 1970s. It lost its world market share dominance and competitiveness during the 1980s to fierce competition from overseas firms in its own domestic markets and global markets. The advent of the 1990s provided a reassessment of its technological competitive position in the global market.

PREPARING FOR THE 21ˢᵗ CENTURY

Silicon Valley began its turnaround in 1993. While some industries and some old firms were still struggling, new industries and new firms were emerging. A 1993 headline in the *San Francisco Chronicle* noted: "Jobs Coming and Going in Silicon Valley." What the article stated was that while some firms, e.g., Apple Computer, were laying off employees, many new companies in emerging networking technologies, SynOptics Communications, for example, were hiring people.[11] Was this an indication of yet another shift to new industries? While semiconductor firms were thriving, computer companies were not doing well. Another local newspaper published data that indicated that U.S. semiconductor firms had regained their lead in chip manufacturing; and Intel Corporation became the largest semiconductor firm in the world, ahead of Japanese firms.[12] This was a remarkable achievement considering that U.S. firms had lost the majority semiconductor market to the Japanese in 1986. In spite of this achievement, a note of caution was added by T.J. Rodgers, President and Chief Executive Officer of Cypress Semiconductor: "There's always the arrogance of success and that's why the Japanese clobbered us in the 1980s. That attitude could come back again."[13]

A report issued by Joint Venture: Silicon Valley in January 1996, noted that Silicon Valley added 46,000 jobs since 1992 with most of the gain coming in software, services, semiconductors, and industrial design.[14] "The improved situation in Silicon Valley has largely been fueled by a fresh infusion of venture capital, which has increased by 48% between 1993 and 1995" to almost $1 billion in 1995.

Silicon Valley firms had a record in revenues and profits in 1995. The sales for the top 150 companies was $142.2 billion with profits of $12.7 billion, according to the annual report published by *San Jose Mercury News* in April 1996.

All this leads to a questioning of this recovery. What factors are causing this revitalization and is it temporary or permanent? Is the recovery caused by economic factors or is it a function of the Silicon Valley firms' response to competitive challenges? If the industry is robust, why are there continued layoffs? Is this the price of productivity gains? According to Jerry Sanders, Chairman and Chief Executive Officer of Advanced Micro Devices: "We were on the rocks. The Japanese forced us to be great. We adapted and we surprised them."[15]

But what about the computer firms? Although the Silicon Valley firms' revenues and profitability are growing, the local economy is still weak and layoffs are continuing in many high-technology firms. What is the real cost of this rejuvenation? James Mitchell, Business Editor of the *San Jose Mercury News*, wrote in an editorial:

As 1994 begins, Silicon Valley's economic
landscape, at first glance, seems to have
changed little from a year ago. While
several of our larger companies face at least
temporary problems. . . . others have done
exceptionally well. On balance, the sales
and earnings of local companies increased
substantially in 1993. The Valley's
employees, however, have done much more
poorly. Changing fortunes, new
technologies and more efficient
management techniques have led so many
companies to lay off workers or restructure
that even those who haven't lost jobs are
looking over their shoulders. High costs,
resource-wasting government bureaucracies
and inadequate local schools continue to put
the Valley at a competitive disadvantage.[16]

Silicon Valley is still a dominant contributor to the U.S.
national economy. While firms may increase revenues, become
competitive worldwide, and even regain world leadership positions, it
follows that the local economy and employment must also improve.
According to Lenny Siegel, Director of Pacific Studies in Mountain
View, California: "The Valley may never return to its fantastic
growth rates of recent economic booms, but it is unlikely to become
an industrial ghost town."

Silicon Valley is at the crossroads today. Though it is doing
well in 1996, its future success is no longer assured. Apple Computer
has demonstrated that even though it created a new personal computer
industry, it cannot compete in the marketplace of today. Not only did
it dramatically change its management in early 1996, it is still
struggling to define its future strategy. New firms that are creating
new industries in Internet applications, like Netscape and Yahoo, are
the Apple of today. Can they meet the same fate of Apple? Silicon
Valley's future in the 21st century depends on its ability to compete
differently in the new global market with different sets of rules and
different management philosophies. It will also have to operate
differently in order to maintain its position as the leader of the
electronics revolution. Much has been written about the decline and

demise of the Valley in various articles and newspaper columns. Some argue that the Valley is not in decline but that it is only adjusting to the new global competitive environment. Its decline is spotlighted in the media because of layoffs referred to as "downsizing," reduction in world marketshare of its products, plant closings, and the inability to put forward new products that would create new markets or imaginative industry as semiconductors did in the 1970s and personal computers did in the 1980s. Though it is still a formidable technology focal point, it is continuously being challenged by both domestic and international firms. The success of Silicon Valley will be challenged in the future.

NOTES

1. Andrew Grove, "Executive Forum: The Future of Silicon Valley," *California Management Review* (Spring 1987), 154.

2. Hanson, *The New Alchemists*, xiv.

3. Michael L. Dertouzous, Richard K. Lester, and Solow M. Robert, *Made in America: Regaining the Productivity Edge* (New York: Harper Perennial, 1989), 248.

4. Andrew Grove, "The Future of the Computer Industry" *California Management Review* (Fall 1990), 155.

5. Dertouzous, *Made in America*, 248.

6. Ibid., 249.

7. George C. Lodge, *Perestroika for America: Restructuring Business-Government Relations for World Competitiveness* (Boston: Harvard Business School Press, 1990), 73.

8. Ken Siegmann, "Silicon Valley Copes With Hard Times," *San Francisco Chronicle*, July 1993, D1 and D2.

9. Michelle Levander, "Electronics Job Loss High," *San Jose Mercury News*, 20 April 1994, 9D and 15D.

10. Ibid., D2.

11. Don Clark, "Jobs Coming and Going in Silicon Valley," *San Francisco Chronicle*, 7 July 1993, E1 and E3.

12. Rebecca Smith, "U.S. regains chip lead," *San Jose Mercury News*, 15 December 1993, 1F and 2F.

13. Ken Siegmann, "U.S. Takes Back Lead in Chips," *San Francisco Chronicle*, December 1993, D1 and D4.

14. John Markoff, "In Silicon Valley, Halcyon Days Are Back," *San Jose Mercury News*, 15 January 1996.

15. Ken Siegmann, "An American Tale of Semi-Success," *San Francisco Chronicle*, 20 December 1993, B1 and B6.

16. James J. Mitchell, "How Silicon Valley can keep from drifting in a sea of change," *San Jose Mercury News*, 2 January 1994, 1E and 8E.

Chapter 3

The Shift in Global Market and Competitive Forces

> Politics, social forces, culture, economic development, psychological attitudes, and historical habits shape the ever-changing surroundings within which the corporation and its managers live and act.
>
> George C. Lodge[1]

If the major characteristics and competitiveness of Silicon Valley have remained the same during the 1970s and 1980s, then its competitive decline must be attributed to a shift in external market economic forces and competitive advantage factors. Global market environment influences business managers' decisions. The inability of the business manager to respond to the global market changes can result in competitive decline.

This chapter examines those external factors that have influenced the growth and decline of Silicon Valley. It begins with a review of competitiveness and examines the global economic transformation.

PERSPECTIVE ON COMPETITIVENESS

Silicon Valley's future success depends on its ability to compete in global markets. During the last decade, much has been written about the United States economy's decline in competitiveness. Many articles have expounded the loss of American competitiveness. Similarly, Silicon Valley firms have also seen the loss of global market share and the decline in competitiveness. Japan-bashing is common as politicians and media across the country sensationalize economic stagnancy, pointing the finger at unfair trade practices. Firms that were known to offer lifetime employment are now laying off people permanently. There are industries in which the United States did lose international competitiveness (such as automobiles and consumer electronics). But, whether the American economy has lost its competitiveness forever, as many prophets of doom suggest, is a question that needs analysis.

The headlines in the *San Francisco Chronicle* announced that "U.S. Living Standard Fell in '90, Report Says."[2] This report, issued by the Council on Competitiveness based in Washington D.C., stated that the standard of living in the United States declined for the first time since 1982. America also lost ground in productivity and investment. Even before the recession that began in July 1991, the American standard of living was growing more slowly than other industrial nations. The American living standard rose by 33 percent from 1972 through 1990, compared with a gain of 80 percent in Japan and 57 percent on average for other industrial nations.

Among the findings of the above report on trade and investment, Germany was the world's leading exporter of manufactured goods in 1990, with sales of $368 billion, followed by the United States' $287 billion and Japan at $282 billion. The United States investment in new factories, machines and equipment in 1990 remained flat at 12.6% of its total economy, the lowest of any seven summit countries, while Japan remained the leader at 23.4%. During the same period, many large American companies announced permanent job cuts and plant closings.

An article in the *San Jose Mercury News* asserted that the end of the recession will not create new jobs. Collaterally some economists suggest that the main message of this recession is that "Americans should rethink decades old expectations about jobs, wealth and economic growth."[3] For Americans it means that job security may not exist and that incomes may actually decline.

An analogous article in the *Economist* questioned America's ability to compete.[4] stating that "prophets of doom are bewailing the decline and fall of American industry. The biggest threat now facing American companies is that businessmen, and policy makers in Washington, will believe them."

Small wonder that numerous headlines such as these have caused Americans to doubt their own competitiveness. The American economy has survived many recessions, but in today's global economy and the transformation into the information age, recessions have a different connotation. During previous recessions, as the economy regenerated, so did employment and economic growth, causing recessions to be seen as minor economic adjustments. In the past, to counter the recession and boost the economy, government initiated tax cuts, lowered interest rates, increased government spending, and offered various incentive plans to increase consumer and business spending. But today, these remedies may not work.

Firstly, the jobs that are lost will not be replaced. Firms laying off thousands of workers will not hire them again, and the jobs are lost permanently. At the same time, many workers do not have transferable skills to meet the changing industrial requirements.

Secondly, the economic resurgence strategies which worked in the past do not work anymore. Tax cuts alone will not do it. Lower interest rates did not boost the economy: capital investment did not increase. Past remedies do not work now because the world economy has changed. Tax cuts may increase disposable income, but that augmentation may be used to purchase foreign made products. Financial markets cross international boundaries, making it very difficult for the United States to apply earlier monetary strategies to revive the economy. However, it is imperative for the United States to retain and maintain its economic competitiveness.

What constitutes competitiveness? There is no universally accepted single measure of competitiveness. Statistics used to compare competitiveness include, but are not limited to: international trade balances, comparative international figures on productivity, standard of living, manufacturing's share of gross national product (GNP), and comparative industry analysis.[5] However, these statistics do not provide a complete picture.

Since there is no single measure, it is appropriate to compare definitions of competitiveness. The 1985 report of the President's Commission on Industrial Competitiveness defines competitiveness as:

> Competitiveness is the degree to which a nation can, under free and fair market conditions, produce goods and services that meet the test of international markets while simultaneously maintaining or expanding the real incomes of its citizens.[6]

This definition identifies two factors: meeting the test of international markets, and maintaining or expanding real incomes. A nation's ability to produce goods and services for domestic and foreign markets partly determines its international competitiveness. During the 1980s, the United States gross domestic product growth was the lowest in comparison to Japan and other newly industrialized countries in Asia (Table 3.1).

TABLE 3.1

GROSS DOMESTIC PRODUCT GROWTH RATES FOR
SELECTED WORLD REGIONS
(annual percentage change in GDP)

Region	1984-88	1989	1990	1991	1992	1993
U.S.	2.6%	1.2%	(0.7%)	2.6%	2.4%	2.8%
Japan	3.8%	4.8%	4.0%	1.3%	0.6%	2.3%
Asia (NICs)	7.3%	7.0%	7.3%	5.2%	5.8%	6.5%

Source: International Monetary Fund, "World Economy Outlook,"
1993.

The concept of "test of international markets" measures the global market share. A nation's exports determine its ability to compete in international markets. The United States was a major export country before the 1970s. Since then, imports into the United

States have exceeded the exports from the United States, with a major increase in imports in the 1980s (Table 3.2).

TABLE 3.2

U.S. IMPORTS AND EXPORTS (1970-1992)
(in billions of dollars)

Year	Exports	Imports
1970	42.7	40.0
1972	49.2	55.6
1974	98.1	102.6
1976	115.2	123.5
1978	143.7	174.8
1980	220.6	244.9
1982	212.3	244.0
1984	217.9	325.7
1986	217.3	370.0
1988	310.0	441.0
1990	393.6	495.3
1991	421.7	487.1
1992	448.2	532.5

Source: U.S. Bureau of the Census.

The most dramatic change occurred in the 1980s when United States firms lost substantial world market share of their products. Between 1980 and 1986, United States exports declined as a percentage of world exports, while the imports increased from 12.5% to 17.5% as a percentage of world imports during the same period (Table 3.3).

TABLE 3.3

U.S. SHARE OF WORLD IMPORTS AND EXPORTS

Year	Percent of Imports	Percent of Exports
1980	12.5	11.1
1982	13.4	11.6
1983	14.4	11.1
1985	17.9	11.1
1986	17.5	10.3

Source: United Nations, Department of International and Social Affairs.[7]

Considered separately, the diminution in world market share is not indicative of a decline in competitiveness. To a degree that was expected because other countries in Europe and Asia improved their economies after the Second World War, the United States market share had to taper off. But, as the American world market share decreased, did the American workers' standard of living improve? The question reflects another competitive issue.

What has happened in the United States is that with the decline in market share, there has also been an accompanying erosion of the real hourly wages of manufacturing workers and all other workers employed in the private sector. The manufacturing wages had peaked to almost $8.65 per hour in 1985 but declined to about $8.00 per hour by 1992. Even the real weekly wages of manufacturing workers, which peaked in the late 1970s, had deteriorated to the levels of the late 1960s (Table 3.4).

TABLE 3.4

AVERAGE HOURLY AND WEEKLY EARNINGS
IN CONSTANT DOLLARS, BY PRIVATE INDUSTRY GROUP

Item	1970	1980	1985	1990	1991	1992
Hourly Mfg.	8.33	8.49	8.65	8.14	8.07	8.03
Total Average	8.03	7.78	7.77	7.52	7.45	7.43
Weekly Mfg.	332	337	350	332	328	329
Total Average	298	275	271	259	256	255

Source: U.S. Bureau of Labor Statistics.

If we define "the test of international competitiveness" and "changes in real income" as measures of decline in economic competitiveness, then the United States has indeed lost competitiveness.

In *Short-Term America*, Michael Jacobs, argues:

> Competitiveness can be measured in a number of ways, but none of them is fully adequate. Economists look to measures such as productivity, investment, per capita income, trade balances, and global market share. Regardless of which yardstick we choose, the story is the same: relative to many Asian and European countries, the United States is losing ground.[8]

The decline of Silicon Valley's competitiveness is attributed to some of these factors. Silicon Valley technology firms saw their market share in semiconductors dwindle from 60 percent in 1980 to 36 percent in 1988, and from 56 percent to 20 percent in DRAMS during the same period.[9]

Competitiveness means different things to different people according to the article in the *Atlantic Monthly*. To American households, it means worrying about the future and affording children's education. To corporations, it means losing market share to foreign firms. To blue-collar workers, it means layoffs and learning new skills, and to Washington, it means "both nothing and everything."[10] While discussing and analyzing competitiveness can be intellectually stimulating, nothing productive usually emerges to deal with the issue. In *Turning the Tables*, Daniel Burnstein states:

> The sad reality is that even though
> "competitiveness" has been a Washington
> buzzword for more than a decade—and
> even though the studies, commissions, and
> specific proposals for reform are legion—it
> is hard to identify a single major U.S.
> government initiative of the 1980s that
> actually resulted in positive change on any
> of the most central structural issues.[11]

To Bruce Scott and George Lodge, two highly-reputed Harvard professors, competitiveness means "the ability to employ U.S. resources, both human resources and capital resources, so that Americans can earn increasing returns while in open competition with other countries."[12] Competitiveness should not be judged only from the past, as those economic figures would indicate, but judged from the present and future perspective.[13] According to them, competitiveness "is more and more a matter of strategies, and less and less a product of natural endowments."[14]

Paul Krugman, a noted MIT economist, states that Americans are obsessed with national competitiveness to the extent "that every country is like a giant corporation slugging it out against rivals in global markets."[15] While companies can cease to exist, nations continue to exist. His premise is that nations should focus on raising domestic productivity, and firms will have to compete globally on their own ability. As he said in *The Age of Diminished Expectations:*

> Productivity isn't everything, but in the
> long run it is almost everything. A
> country's ability to improve its standard of
> living over time depends almost entirely on
> its ability to raise its output per worker.[16]

Similarly, Silicon Valley's ability to compete globally will depend on its ability to improve productivity in the face of changing market and technological conditions.

THE SHIFT IN MARKET ECONOMIC FORCES

During the relatively short history of Silicon Valley, world economic relationships changed. As nations and firms competed earlier against each other through their domestic strengths, today the world economies are interdependent and firms are global, competing for resources and markets worldwide in what is a truly global economy.

As the world continues to move towards globally interdependent economies, intense global competition, and market driven economies, businesses and industries worldwide face tremendous challenges to survive beyond the second millennium.

American industrial achievements have symbolized the success of the free-enterprise capitalistic system for more than a century. After the second world war, U.S. businesses dominated and controlled the entire free world. As other nations, particularly in Europe and the Far East, grew economically, they were able to transform and integrate American management theories and practices consistent with their unique political, cultural and social environments, and were exceedingly successful in competing against the United States in both global and American markets. While some Far East and European economies grew at unprecedented growth rates, the American economy had a much slower growth rate during the last decade; and in some key industries, it regressed substantially.

In his best selling book *Head to Head*, Lester Thurow states, "In the past half century the world has shifted from being a single polar economic world revolving around the United States to a tripolar world built upon Japan, the European Community, and the United States."[17] He contends that necessary changes will be difficult for the United States because "after World War II the United States did not have economic competitors. It stood alone with effortless economic superiority, playing a game designed to fit its strength."[18] But during the next century, the U.S. "will be just one of a number of equal players playing a game where the rules increasingly will be written by others."[19] That forebodes a formidable adjustment for U.S.

businesses. Nevertheless, American management will have to adjust to the new economic world order and unlearn some of its former business practices.

Another perspective on the changing world economy is provided by Peter Drucker in his book *Managing for the Future* in which he states that with OPEC and President Nixon's floating of the dollar in the mid-1970s, "the world economy changed from international to transnational. The transnational economy is shaped mainly by the dynamics of money flows rather than goods and services."[20] The goal of management in a transnational enterprise, according to Drucker, "is maximization of market share, not the traditional short-term 'profit maximization' of the old style corporation.[21]

During the 1950s, American businesses dominated world industrial production and the United States enjoyed a per capita GNP four times that of West Germany and 15 times that of Japan.[22] This was possible because those countries were economically devastated. Economically, American exports were not a threat to those countries. The United States was exporting agricultural products, raw materials, and technology related products that the other nations needed or did not have.[23] It was a desirable business environment for the U.S. and acceptable to other countries.

At the beginning of 1990, according to the *Economist*, the per capita GNP in external purchasing power of Japan and Germany was larger than that of the United States.[24] The United States was no longer the lead nation in all industries. In automobiles, the United States is now a follower; and in consumer electronics it is no longer even a contender. In 1970, American firms accounted for 64 of the top 100 in the world. By 1990, that number had declined to 42.[25] The American firms did not have to face stiff foreign competition until the 1970s. Between 1972 and 1982, "the proportion of American-made goods subject to international competition jumped from 20 to 80 percent."[26]

Many economists argue that the U.S. still possesses the overall industrial lead. In total economic terms it does, but in the industries of the future, including microelectronics, biotechnology, the new material-sciences, telecommunications, civil aviation, robotics, and machine tools, it is declining.[27]

The *Economist*, in a 1992 feature article on "Survey of America" defined the global economic success of the United States after World War II as an "aberration of history" because it was the sole economic power, with very limited worldwide competition.[28] It is rare that a nation faces no economic competition.

In addition to the above competitive factors, earlier American economic success, according to Lester Thurow, can also be attributed to the following four factors:[29]

1. Abundance of raw materials.
2. Relatively small population in a resource rich environment.
3. Implementation of a compulsory education system.
4. Development of a mass higher education system.

But today's business environment is different. The four factors that enabled the U.S. to do well in the past have lost their relevance. The reasons for the new scenario are:[30]

- Natural resources no longer assure economic success. The advances in biotechnology and material sciences has made that possible. Japan has no resources, but it is rich. Argentina has an abundance of resources, but it is not a rich country. Raw materials account for less and less toward the total cost of the product, and materials today account for less than 40% of product cost; and it continues to contract.
- Management depends on availability of capital for financing operations. Today, capital is available throughout the world. Among the top 20 banks in the world in 1990, there were no American banks. Businesses in Japan and Germany now have the same easy access to money worldwide as does any American concern. American firms now have to compete for capital, and their performance is judged according to international standards.
- Technology has changed the concept of industries from labor and materials intensive to "knowledge" intensive. Brainpower industries can be located anywhere in the world aided by advanced communications and computer networks. Local presence is no longer required. Today, many firms have research and development groups in countries other than their own. The declining product life cycles have necessitated increased investment in research and process development.
- Skills required of people have changed. Peter Drucker describes the future worker as the "knowledge worker," the term he coined in

1960. The blue collar mentality in the United States, where the focus was on mastering one task, has changed. Those tasks are now transferred to low-skill and low-wage countries or to robots, while the developed countries focus on "knowledge work." The new skills required of the labor force place a heavy training burden on American managers to meet the new economic reality.

This new economic reality changed the old concept of complementary and competitive trade to adversarial trade. Drucker explains: "Complementary trade sought a partnership. Competitive trade sought a customer. Adversarial trade aims to dominate entire industries."[31]

Many American corporations and industries are facing onerous times due to their lack of appropriate responses to the changing global economic competitive environment. Giant companies, such as General Motors, IBM, Chrysler, Sears, Data General, Wang, and Digital Equipment, which were successful just a few years ago, are now struggling to survive or are out of business. They are victims of the new world order that they helped create in the first place.

NOTES

1. George C. Lodge and Ezra F. Vogel eds., *Ideology and National Competitiveness: An Analysis of Nine Countries* (Boston: Harvard Business School Press, 1987), 1.

2. *San Francisco Chronicle*, Fall 1991.

3. *San Jose Mercury News*, 17 November 1991.

4. *The Economist* (London), 18 January 1992.

5. Congress of the United States, Office of Technology Assessment, *Competing Economies: America, Europe, and the Pacific Rim*, (Washington D.C.: Government Printing Office, 1991), 3.

6. Ibid., 3.

7. Ibid., 3.

8. Michael T. Jacobs, *Short-Term America: The Causes and Cures of Our Business Myopia* (Boston: Harvard Business School Press, 1991), 2.

9. Ibid., 4.

10. Peter G. Peterson, "The Morning After," *The Atlantic Monthly*, October 1987, 43.

11. Daniel Burnstein, *Turning the Tables: A Machiavellian Strategy for Dealing with Japan* (New York: Simon and Schuster, 1993), 45.

12. Bruce R. Scott and George C. Lodge, *U.S. Competitiveness in the World Economy* (Boston: Harvard Press, 1985), 3.

13. Ibid., 4.

14. Ibid., 5.

15. Paul Krugman, "Competitiveness: Does it Matter?" *Fortune*, 7 March 1994, 109.

16. Paul Krugman, *The Age of Diminished Expectations: U.S. Economic Policy in the 1990s* (Cambridge: The MIT Press, 1990), 9.

17. Lester Thurow, *Head to Head: The Coming Economic Battle Among Japan, Europe, and America* (New York: William Morrow and Co., 1992), 15.

18. Ibid., 16.

19. Ibid., 17.

20. Peter F. Drucker, *Managing for the Future: The 1990s and Beyond* (New York: Truman Talley/Dutton, 1992), 8.

21. Ibid., 8.

22. Thurow, *Head to Head*, 29.

23. Ibid., 29.
24. *Economist* (London), 1992.
25. Thurow, *Head to Head*, 29 and 30.
26. Burnstein, *Turning the Tables*, 2.
27. Ibid., 30.
28. *Economist*, (London) 26 October 1991.
29. Thurow, *Head to Head*, 40.
30. Ibid., 40-55.
31. Drucker, *Managing for the Future*, 7.

Chapter 4

Ideology and Global Competition

The ideological evolution of the American corporation has played a predominant role in current American business practices. The inability to respond to the new global economic order may be attributed to its history of evolution and its national ideology.

THE EVOLUTION OF THE AMERICAN CORPORATION

The foundation for the evolution of American ideology can be traced to the historical development of the nation. Immigrants, who had left Europe to seek their fortunes in America, were endeavoring to carve a nation out of the vast resource rich land. The frontier spirit relied on individual fulfillment and self-reliant struggle. The United States Constitution spelled out individual rights, and the role of the government became that of protecting the rights of the individual and later, to protect the corporation. Adam Smith's model of capitalism, which emphasized that "each individual's use of property for his own self-interest would help make the good community,"[1] was adopted. He emphasized competition in which the property owners would compete to satisfy individual consumer needs in the marketplace. This ideology founded the growth of American business through individual effort. This ideology also led to the development of the United States as the largest economy in the world.

The development of the American corporation is a symbol of its economic power. During the nineteenth century, in the United States, national identity and interests were equated with economic power. Teddy Roosevelt emphasized the concept that the national economy signified the nation's strength and determination. As Robert Reich, in his bestseller *The Work of Nations*, states: " 'Great power' became synonymous with 'great economy'."[2]

The development of mass-volume manufacturing during the last century converted the population from an agricultural society, where each individual worked on the land for his own survival, to the industrial society, drawing people from farms to cities, thereby creating a new national identity rather than an individual identity. This mass gathering of new workers created the need for new types of organizations. The business corporation was born, fueled by the national desire to develop a strong economy. Thus the American corporation and national economy became synonymous with national welfare and interests.

American business expanded domestically by blocking foreign imports through imposition of high tariffs.[3] It influenced business expansion in other world regions through the World Bank and International Monetary Fund. Robert Reich describes: "Here was the final plank of economic nationalism: The well-being of citizens was linked to the success of the national economy, which depended in turn on the success of its giant corporations."[4] This caused merger-mania among corporations. As corporations grew stronger in power, there arose a mistrust of them. As far back as the colonial period, Americans had "learned to distrust monopolies, special charters, and other royal prerogatives."[5] However, consolidation of corporations continued; and companies that evolved included U.S. Steel, American Telephone & Telegraph, American Rubber, American Can, General Electric, and Standard Oil. Mr. Reich summarized merger and consolidation succinctly: "In short, the giant American corporation was the vehicle by which the resources of the American economy were to be mobilized and directed."[6]

The question of how to control these large corporations persisted in the mind of the nation. Herbert Croly, in *The Promise of American Life*, published in 1909, argued that "the large American corporation should be regulated by the nation and directed towards national goals."[7] Theodore Roosevelt put that into practice, and Americans saw the success of national corporate planning during World War I.

As the strength of American corporations grew, it became more difficult to monitor the accountability of the top executives of these corporations. In the book, "The Modern Corporation and

Private Property," by A.A. Berle and G.C. Means, published in 1932, the authors contended that:

> The top executives of America's giant companies, who controlled the nation's most important economic resources and received most of the government's largesse, were not even accountable to their own shareholders. Executives operated corporations in their own interests, and diverted a portion of the asset fund to their own uses.[8]

This statement is also relevant today in connection with most American corporations. The role of the American executive became that of a "corporate statesmen," who "was responsible for balancing the claims of stockholders, employees, and the American public."[9] This fundamental philosophy of American corporations laid the foundation for the evolution of current American management thinking.

After World War II, "the well-being of individual citizens, the prosperity of the nation, and the success of the nation's core corporations seemed inextricably connected."[10] To ensure their continued dominance, American corporations launched a massive public relations campaign "promoting the wonders of the profit system."[11]

Americans blindly bought the concept of the free enterprise capitalistic system. Prosperity during the 1950s erased any doubt in the minds of American people about the viability of the system, and supported the bigness of the American corporation. Those Americans who had seen the depression era and the two World Wars, were inspirited with this economic growth. David Lilienthal, in his 1953 book *Big Business: A New Era*, stated that "Our productive and distributive superiority, our economic fruitfulness, rest upon Bigness."[12] During the same year, *Fortune* magazine, in an opinion survey, reported that a "vast majority of Americans approved of big business," and concluded that:

> The huge, publicly-owned corporation has become the most important phenomenon of

> mid-century capitalism. Corporate bigness
> is coming to be accepted as an integral part
> of a big economy. Whatever attacks may be
> made against them in theory, the large
> corporations have met the test of delivering
> the goods."[13]

What this commentary did not consider was that, after World War II, the other major economies were shattered and there was limited competition confronting American firms. While other nations were concentrating on building or rebuilding their countries and new infrastructures, American corporations were capitalizing on its economic and manufacturing strength.

The American corporations created a "consumption society." The growth and the growing prosperity of the middle-class developed an unprecedented desire to consume. According to Robert Reich, "Americans took it as their patriotic duty to consume, and understood the purpose of the American economy as enabling them to do so."[14]

The success of the American corporation during the 1950s and 1960s gave a sense of false security and superiority to the American manager. Robert Reich aptly described this arrogance:

> Because of their size and central role in
> the economy, America's core corporations
> came to identify themselves, and be
> identified by Americans and others around
> the world, with the American economy as a
> whole. They were the champions of the
> national economy; their successes were its
> successes. They were the American
> economy.[15]

In an ever-expanding, consumption-oriented society, Americans prospered through the growing purchasing power of the white and blue-collars. This represented one of American capitalism's greatest triumphs. A similar scenario is now playing in Japan and Germany, with both a growing and prosperous middle-class and well-paid factory workers. This economic attainment in Far East Asia and Europe has created new decidedly competitive markets as well as knowledgeable consumers.

The same efficacious organizational approach which caused American firms to succeed in the past, the same organization approach would also lead to their decline in the new world order. American management methodized business much the same as military bureaucracy "for the efficient implementation of preconceived plans."[16] Firms had correspondent military type hierarchies, chains of command, spans of control, job classifications, and standard operating procedures. The main emphasis was on maintaining control and implementation of specific plans. Established production goals and sales quotas were the objectives. The types of top executives that emerged had similar backgrounds, were mostly financially-oriented, went to the same Ivy league schools, had membership in comparable clubs, and circulated in similar social circles. Layers of middle-management were created whose main function was to transmit information upward and downward. The American corporation was creating an "organization man" whose task was to only perform but not to think or create.[17] In his book, *The Lonely Crowd*, David Riesman describes this "faceless" and "other-directed" organization man evolving from the conformity and tractability of standardized, high-volume production. "The system neither required nor rewarded much in the way of original thought."[18]

As part of the unfolding of the management organization, the American corporation created the "foot-soldier" or blue-collar worker who was protected by strong labor unions. During the 1950s and 1960s, about 70% of the American factory workers belonged to some variety of labor union.[19] At the bargaining tables, management and labor agreed upon wage and benefit increase and passed on the increases to the consumer through higher prices. The automobile industry was the quintessential example of this practice. What the firms were ignoring was that if the increases in wages were not supported by increases in productivity, then other firms would become a major competitive threat.

America was not a major trading country during the 1950s. By 1960, it imported less than 4 percent of automobiles, 4 percent of steel, and less than 6 percent of consumer electronics, and only 3 percent of machine tools.[20] Under the aegis of fighting the spread of communism, America exported its model of capitalism to the rest of the world. They manipulated the World Bank into financing projects in those regions of the world that would benefit American firms.[21]

However, while American corporations exported products worldwide, they also exported marketing skills, technologies, manufacturing plants, distribution techniques, and management styles. It was not anticipated that the other regions would not only learn from the American capitalistic model, but would also easily adapt it to their own cultural and economic conditions and beat the American corporations at their own game. Robert Reich confirmed: "It was only a matter of time before American manufacturing know-how, arcing out into the postwar world, would come around full circle to where it began, like a giant boomerang."[22] In less than two decades, foreign firms mastered advanced manufacturing and sold higher quality and less expensive products in the United States; and American consumers readily accepted cheaper and better foreign products. American companies were heedless of the consequences, or chose to ignore the threat, for it was inconceivable to American firms that any other country could build better products. What shocked the American corporations was that foreigners "could build and manage modern factories as effectively as could the executives of Americans' national champions."[23] By the 1960s, American firms were subject to fierce foreign competition.

The American corporation's response was typical. It went to the government to create barriers: the same approach tried a hundred years ago. According to International Trade Commission, by the end of the 1980s, "almost a third of the standard goods manufactured in the United States, by value, were protected against international competition."[24]

The second response was to establish factories overseas to take advantage of cheap labor, much to the discomfort of the American worker. By now, the American corporation was thinking of its survival and profitability and not of the national interest that had propelled the American corporation into business during the last century.

The third response was the manipulation of financial results through acquisitions, mergers, junk-bonds, and other financial means to show the financial strength of the company. None of these was increasing the competitive strength of the corporation. Selfish interests ruled the corporations, and attaining of individual wealth among the key managers became the top priority.

A basic contention is that the development and evolution of the American corporation as described above has created the practice of

American management. The concept of budgeting, financial controls, management by objectives, rate of return analysis, and various quantitative analytical techniques are all by-products of the American management and economic system. Economists, like Milton Friedman in his article "The Social Responsibility of Business Is to Increase Its Profits," espoused that the only purpose of a business is to maximize profits. If the American manager desires to change, it must be through active participation in changing the management system before global competitiveness can be achieved. Using occasional Japanese and German management techniques will not be adequate to accomplish this purpose. Further, the concepts of Theory Z, Quality Circles, or Just-in-time manufacturing have not worked in the American system because the evolution of the management systems in Japan and Germany is quite different than that in the United States; and resorting to quick-fix techniques is not the answer. The American, Japanese, and German approaches to their business environments are different due to dissimilar economic, political, and cultural systems. If lessons are to be learned by American managers, they will also have to understand the nature of Japanese and German business evolutions.

THE ROLE OF IDEOLOGY IN GLOBAL COMPETITION

The evolution of management ideology is based on cultural, national, social, political, and religious characteristics of each region. In the book, *Managing Across Borders*, the authors state:

> The influence of a nation's history, infrastructure, and cultural permeates all aspects of life within the country, including the norms, values, and behaviors of managers in its national companies. Nationally influenced behavioral characteristics become an ingrained part of each company's "way of doing things" and shape its international organization structure and processes.[25]

American managers have always equated the past success of the American economy to its free-enterprise capitalistic system. Firms are free to compete freely with each other and with other firms in the world, and the firm with the best and most economic product gains the victory. The recent downfall of the communist system reinforced the superiority of the American capitalistic system. When American managers criticized the Japanese for unfair trade practices, they were partly critical of the Japanese capitalistic system. The capitalistic system in Japan and Germany is not identical to the American capitalistic system. To Americans, all capitalistic systems are alike and are based on the American model. When comparing the American with the Japanese and German management systems, it is imperative to understand how the ideologies of each nation have shaped their business philosophies.

Each nation has its own ideology. George Lodge defines ideology as "a set of beliefs and assumptions about values that the nation holds to justify and make legitimate the actions and purpose of its institutions."[26] Japan, with limited land, is wholly dependent on the outside world for its natural resources, and, therefore, developed a different ideology for its economic survival than did the nineteenth century United States where a sparse population had abundant land and natural resources. Once these ideologies are established over decades or centuries, they are not easy to change. The two ideologies that are prevalent in the modern capitalistic world are "individualism" and "communitarianism."[27] U.S. practices individualistic capitalism while Japan and Germany both practice communitarianism capitalism. The two systems are defined in *Ideology and National Competitiveness:*

> Individualism suggests an atomistic conception of society, one in which the individual is the ultimate source of value and meaning. The interests of the community are defined and achieved by self-interested competition among many, preferably small, proprietors. Communitarianism, however, takes a more organic view, regarding the community as more than the sum of its individuals and

requiring explicit definition of its needs and priorities.[28]

The individualistic ideology has five components with individual rights as the driving factor. This concept of American individualism is best explained by Alexis de Tocqueville in his classic book *Democracy in America* written in 1825:

> 'Individualism' is a word recently coined to express a new idea . . . it is a calm and considered feeling which disposes each citizen to isolate himself from the mass of his fellows and withdraw into a circle of family and friends; with this little society formed to his taste, he gladly leaves the greater society to look after itself.[29]

The other characteristic of the individualism is the emphasis on property rights of the individual. By giving the individual "sanctity of property rights" he is assured "freedom from the predatory powers of the state; and from this notion the corporate manager derives the authority to manage."[30] Adam Smith further enforced the idea of competition to meet consumer desire, and the individual was free to pursue intense competition to further his or her well-being. In order to pursue individual success, the powers of the government were supposed to be limited and government intervention in the free-enterprise system was considered an invasion of the individual rights. Less government was desirable.

In contrast, communitarian ideology is "characterized by equality of result or hierarchy, and consensus, which may be coerced or arrived at more or less voluntarily."[31] The community "is more than the sum of the individuals."[32] As stated by George Lodge:

> The community as a whole has special and urgent needs that go beyond the needs of its individual members. The values of survival, justice, self-respect, and so forth, depend on the recognition of those needs.[33]

Other characteristics of the communitarian system detail the rights and duties of the membership in the community that each individual inhabits. Property rights may be superseded by the rights of the welfare of the society. The needs of the survival of the community are stressed and clearly identified. The state is an active participant in the planning process and works closely with industry for economic growth. There also exists a sense of "holism"[34] or interdependence where there is a demand for cooperation between man and nature.

How does this apply to the workings of the American, German, and Japanese systems? Lester Thurow, in his book *Head to Head* explains the manifestations of these ideologies. He states:

> America and Britain trumpet individualistic values: the brilliant entrepreneur, Nobel Prize winners, large wage differentials, individual responsibility for skills, easy to fire and easy to quit, and hostile mergers and take-overs—their hero is the Lone Ranger. In contrast, Germany and Japan trumpet communitarian values: business groups, social responsibility for skills, teamwork, firm loyalty, industry strategies, and active industrial policies that promote growth. Anglo-Saxon firms are profit maximizers; Japanese business firms play a game that might be better known as 'strategic conquest.' Americans believe in "consumer economics"; Japanese believe in "producer economics."[35]

He further explains that in the American capitalistic system:

> The individual is supposed to have a personal economic strategy for success, and the business firm is supposed to have an economic strategy that is a reflection of the wishes of the individual shareholders. Since shareholders want income to maximize their

lifetime consumption, their firms must be
profit maximizers. For the profit-
maximizing firm, customer and employee
relations are merely a means to the end of
higher profits for the shareholders. Wages
are to be beaten down where possible, and
when not needed, employees are to be laid
off.[36]

However, in the communitarian capitalistic system, the
individual is part of a team and wants to make the team successful. In
Japan, the first responsibility of the firm is to the employees, second
to the customers, and the shareholders are a distant third. Profits are
frequently sacrificed to maintain wages and employment. During
periods of hardship, senior management makes the initial sacrifice. At
the same time, management is prevented from "engaging in self-
serving activities such as poison pills or golden parachutes that do not
enhance the company's long-term prospects."[37]

While American business practices have been influenced by the
philosophy of Adam Smith, Japanese and German ideologies have
been shaped by the work of Friedrich List, a German economist. In
his book *The National System of Political Economy*, published in
1841, he espoused that the government should support their industrial
growth through a system of tariffs, subsidies, and other protectionist
policies.[38] Therein lies the basis of conflict between American and
Japanese economic practices. According to Paul Krugman, Western
economists did not realize the discrepancies between their economic
theory and global reality till the mid-1980s.[39]

The Japanese Adaptive Communitarian Capitalism

Modern Japanese business ideology has its foundation during
the Tokugawa regimes starting in the 1600s. Tokugawa leaders
encouraged learning as a path to governing. Ezra Vogel, in his article,
"Adaptive Communitarian" describes the emerging ideology:

Tokugawa leaders believed that loyalty and
service, a sense of responsibility, and a
respect for discipline, training, and

craftsmanship were necessary to provide a
stable basis for political order.[40]

The active role of government in business emerged in 1858
during the Meiji Period when Japan decided to open its doors to the
outside world. To modernize and compete with the industrial
revolution evolving in Europe and America, the Japanese government
sent its representatives abroad to explore technologies that would
allow development of a modern industrial economy. However, most
of the traditional merchants and businessmen did not have the
necessary capital needed to modernize. Government-supported
regional banks emerged during the 1870s to provide the necessary
capital to further those industries that would accelerate the
development of Japan as a whole. Government became an active
business sponsor and partner; and the involvement continues to exist
today through the support of Ministry of International Trade and
Industry (MITI) and through the Ministry of Finance. Although
government assisted the industries, and in some cases even
participated in starting them, it would not run them and sold those
industries at a very low price to private parties. Mr. Vogel explains:

> The very first large industries were
> developed in the 1870s. Some began as
> government corporations, but in 1881 they
> were sold at a relatively low cost to private
> companies. Although the government had
> ended its support of these companies to
> meet a financial crisis, another principle
> underlay its move: some basic industries
> might require government help to start or
> government models to teach them new
> ways, but they would prosper better and
> grow under private enterprise. Thus the
> decision to let some companies go private
> was made for communitarian reasons, an
> ideological basis very different from that
> for private property in the United States
> and Europe. The purchasers of these
> companies knew from the beginning that

their success depended in part on the initial
assistance given them by the government.[41]

The ideology of sacrificing profits for long-term economic
stability was echoed by Eichi Shibusawa, a financier, in 1890: "This
enterprise should not be looked upon from the angle of profit-making
alone but for the good of the country."[42] Since the inception of the
Meiji regime, it was acceptable for the corporations to make a profit,
but they owed their primary responsibility to the national and social
interests. In essence, "large companies created with government
assistance were not privately-owned but were operated for national
purposes."[43]

During the Meiji regime, the entire focus of the Japanese
government was to learn and acquire industrial know-how from
abroad. There was no interest in international trade. Mr. Vogel
describes the Japanese business acumen:

> In line with the traditional neo-
> Confucian value placed on learning, early
> leaders of Meiji searched throughout the
> world for the best ideas and most modern
> technology to stimulate and modernize their
> nation so that they might avoid being
> colonized by foreigners. . . . Japanese
> leaders then began a systematic and careful
> introduction of new systems in all fields:
> government, administration, business
> organization, banking, military, education,
> local government, agriculture, and
> commerce.[44]

This ideology still exists in Japan. Japanese businesses are open to
new ideas and suggestions and are not afraid to engage in or copy
foreign techniques. An evidential example is the acquisition of
transistor technology by Akio Morita of Sony who created a whole
new industry using transistors in miniaturizing radios. Another
American adaptation is Japanese application of America's Deming's
quality techniques while American companies ignored his concepts.

Since the early Meiji Period, the Japanese companies invested
heavily in employee training and education, thus developing loyal

work forces and promoting the concept of teamwork and consensus management. The adaptation of Western management in Japan is explained by Vogel:

> When the Japanese began learning from the West, they took institutions that they thought would benefit the nation as a whole. They eagerly brought in modern factories, corporations, banks, universities, army, and navy. They tried to avoid lawyers of the Western sort, who created greater divisiveness in society and tended to pull it apart. They avoided excessive concern with individual rights and due process, both of which they believed would make it difficult for organizations to look out for the overall order.[45]

Referral to the concept of teamwork, participative management, consensus building, and implementation of these in American businesses, tends to overlook the fact that the Japanese work well together "because they were trained as children to enjoy the benefits of cooperation . . . and because they believe that the fate of everyone living on the Japanese islands is closely bound together."[46]

The success of Japanese businesses during the last few decades is not a fluke, but is based on the strong ideology of its people and the institutions which have evolved during the last four hundred years.

The German Competing Communitarianism Capitalism

Although Germany is considered in accord with Western philosophical thinking, its business ideology is not similar to that of United States. It is somewhere between that of Japan and the United States. During the past two centuries, the business ideology in Germany has been influenced by its institutions and social organizations. As in Japan, the leaders in government, business, and labor have termed the welfare of the community their first priority.

Germany's economic thinking has been influenced by the writings of the German philosopher, I. He argued that "only through a strong state could individuals find fulfillment."[47] Germany was slow to industrialize during the last century in comparison to Great Britain and the United States. Analogous with Japan, support was sought from the government to catch up with the industrialized countries. Unlike Japan, the initial flow of capital came from the British, which subsequently led to the development of German investment banks. Since then, German banks have played a major role in the development of German industries. As in Japan, "organized capitalism"[48] was being created, unlike American capitalism which evolved without government intervention. Because Germany had the socialistic thinking foundation of Marx and Hegel, labor unions had a strong influence in the growth of industrial Germany. The labor union is still a strong force in Germany, but unlike American labor unions, it has the welfare of the German nation as the main concern. The socialist influence during Bismarck's rule created a structure for social insurance and welfare programs. As of today, Germany has a strong welfare and training support program for its working class. The German apprentice training program is a model for many nations.

Germany, a land with limited natural resources, relied heavily on exports for its economic growth. In his article "Germany: Communitarian Capitalism," Christopher Allen states:

> Economic competition in Germany has always been intimately bound up with the international issues of obtaining sufficient natural resources and gaining access to world markets. The heavy dependence on the nation's large corporations on exports made it essential that industry work closely with the banks and the state to better Germany's international position.[49]

The present role of the government is a policy "framing" one, setting monetary and fiscal policies that allow the private sector to compete internationally. According to Mr. Allen:

> Regulation in Germany always has some strategic national purpose: an active labor-market policy to smooth the movement of workers from one industry to another; the development of a craft-based

> apprenticeship system to maintain needed
> skilled workers; and the funding of a
> ministry of research and technology to help
> industry develop promising new
> products . . . German business does not
> adopt an antagonistic attitude towards these
> measures because it perceives that the
> state's regulation is undertaken for the
> long-run economic good of the firm or
> industry.[50]

The main feature of the German system is its investment in the skills of its work force, supported by the government, business, and labor. In the United States skill training is mostly left to the individual. Today, Germany has one of the largest economies in the world, with an extremely skilled and advanced labor force, and with an impressively successful experience in exports.

How ideologies have shaped business practices in the United States, Japan, and Germany is evident by the fact that Germans are "good at building infrastructures, Americans excel at invention, and Japanese excel at innovation of getting new products to market."[51]

The American Management Orthodoxy

The American ideology worked especially well until about 30 years ago. The U.S. was the dominant economic force creating new products and technologies. However, as the economies of Europe and the Far East began to grow, foreign firms began to compete aggressively with American firms in the United States and international markets. American firms lost market shares in many industries. Many American firms tried emulating Japanese management styles and techniques. However, most American companies failed in these imitation programs. In an enlightening article in the Harvard Business Review, Hayes and Abernathy identified the reasons for our economic decline, reasons attributed to the American ideology. They blamed the decline on three different management orthodoxies: financial controls, corporate portfolio management, and market-driven behavior.[52]

The concept of financial controls measures the firm as a profit center. As long as it is making money, it remains a viable venture.

Performance is measured in terms of return on investment. The process is controlled through budgets, financial plans and objectives. Executives focus on short-term financial success to achieve their individual bonuses and thus retaining stockholders satisfaction. The financial controls ignore the long-term viability or investment of the firm. Long-term strategic development is sacrificed for short-term profits.

The portfolio management concept emphasizes the measurement of a business from the risk and return analysis. Thus risk avoidance is emphasized for the sake of returns. A business that does not provide acceptable rates of return is discarded, although it may be the business of the future, may have a great technology, or a greatly talented group of people. The business is treated as a financial entity and not as a future growth venture.

In market-driven behavior, American companies are product-oriented bent on satisfying existing consumer needs. Market-oriented firms create new products which create new markets. This approach requires investment, innovation, and risk.

According to the authors, the decline of American business competitiveness is rooted in our American ideology; emphasizing short-term profits. While these managerial orthodoxies may have worked thirty years ago when American firms serviced and competed in domestic markets almost single-handedly, that is not the case today. Additionally, competing in the future will "require some fundamental changes in management attitudes and practices."[53]

NOTES

1. George C. Lodge and Ezra F. Vogel, *Ideology and National Competitiveness* (Boston: Harvard Business School, 1987), 105.

2. Robert Reich, *The Work of Nations: Preparing Ourselves for 21st Century Capitalism* (New York: Alfred A. Knopf, 1992), 30.

3. Ibid., 20.

4. Ibid., 34.

5. Ibid., 35.

6. Ibid., 37.

7. Ibid., 39.

8. Ibid., 41.

9. Ibid., 42.

10. Ibid., 43.

11. Ibid., 43.

12. Ibid., 44.

13. Ibid., 44.

14. Ibid., 45.

15. Ibid., 47.

16. Ibid., 51.

17. William H. Whyte, Jr., *The Organization Man* (New York: Simon & Schuster, 1956).

18. David Riesman, *The Lonely Crowd: A Study of the Changing American Character* (New York: Doubleday, 1950), 151-60.

19. Reich, *The Work of Nations*, 55.

20. Ibid., 63.

21. Ibid., 64.

22. Ibid., 69.

23. Ibid., 70.

24. Ibid., 71.

25. Christopher A. Bartlett and Sumantra Ghoshal, *Managing Across Borders* (Boston: Harvard Business School Press, 1990), 42.

26. George C. Lodge and Ezra F. Vogel, eds., *Ideology and National Competitiveness: An Analysis of Nine Countries* (Boston: Harvard Business School Press, 1987), 2.

27. Ibid., 9.

28. Ibid., 9.

29. Alexis de Tocqueville, *Democracy in America* (New York: Mentor Book, 1956), 193.
30. Lodge, Ideology and National Competitiveness, 12.
31. Ibid., 14.
32. Ibid., 15.
33. Ibid., 15.
34. Ibid., 21.
35. Thurow, Head to Head, 32.
36. Ibid., 32.
37. Ibid., 35.
38. San Francisco Chronicle, 28 February 1994.
39. Lodge, Perestroika for America, 17.
40. Lodge, Ideology and National Competitiveness, 142.
41. Ibid., 147-8.
42. Ibid., 148.
43. Ibid., 148.
44. Ibid., 150.
45. Ibid., 153.
46. Ibid., 156.
47. Ibid., 81.
48. Ibid., 81.
49. Ibid., 87.
50. Ibid., 88.
51. Charles Hampden-Turner and Alfons Trompenaars, Seven Cultures of Capitalism (New York: Doubleday, 1993), 3.
52. Robert H. Hayes and William J. Abernathy, "Managing our way to economic decline," Harvard Business Review (July-August 1980): 70.
53. Ibid., 77.

Chapter 5

The Relevance of Comparative Advantage Theory

> Comparative advantage is better ideas, more promptly acted upon, better devised for more rapid manufacture, more vigorously marketed, adapted faster by learning from real-life customers, with the resulting knowledge applied as even better ideas, more ingenious inventions, more flexible human systems-a continuous spiral of enterprise in which no one is ever dependably ahead for long.
>
> Harlan Cleveland[1]

The concept of comparative advantage has altered during the last two decades. The economic advantage that a given nation or industry naturally possessed, either through its natural resource or particular skill, may not be applicable in today's global economy. While the competitive advantage of many industries in the past was due to the easy availability of raw materials, labor, capital or other resources, today's industries compete by creating new comparative advantages, irrespective of whether they are endowed with any natural advantages. This is a new paradigm for business and industry.

THEORY OF COMPARATIVE ADVANTAGE

Nations trade. What, why, and when nations trade determines the economic well-being of a nation. In 1776, Adam Smith, in his famous book *The Wealth of Nations*, explained the concept of absolute advantage. He theorized "that national real income could be maximized if a country specialized in its export sector and imported only those goods that others could make for less."[2] If a nation could produce a good cheaper than other country, then it had an absolute advantage. The nation would benefit for it would produce goods "because of natural and acquired advantages."[3]

David Ricardo challenged Smith's theory in 1817. According to Ricardo, "incentives for trade existed even when one country held an absolute cost advantage in all goods."[4] Specialization maximized both the trading nations. In his principle of comparative advantage, Ricardo states:

A nation, like a person, gains from trade by exporting the goods or services in which it has its greatest comparative advantage in productivity and importing those in which it has the least comparative advantage.[5]

The theory is based on important assumptions: "full employment, balanced current accounts, the existence of productive factors that are 'homogeneous and mobile between sectors' and which can thus 'costlessly be reallocated from one sector to another,' and the comparability of knowledge and technology from one country to another."[6]

Subsequently, many refinements were added to Ricardo's theory. Eli Heckscher and later Bertil Ohlin expounded the factor proportions theory of international trade, in which countries export those goods that utilize the "country's most abundant factors of production."[7] This became known as the Heckscher-Ohlin (H-O) theory. However, Wassily Leontief published data in the mid-1950s "showing that U.S. exports were less capital-intensive than were U.S. imports,"[8] contradicting H-O theory. Many economists attempted to explain the Leontief paradox. Some economists, including Irving Kravis and Donald Keesing argued that the United States had an educated, skilled labor force and if human capital were added to the value of physical capital then the paradox could be explained. Other economists, William Gruber and Ramond Vernon, for example, "stressed that the United States gained an efficiency advantage from its R&D-oriented industries."[9] Still others tried to explain the paradox through evaluating natural resource endowments, internal demand, product life cycles, and intra-industry trade. Nevertheless, the debate on why, what, and when nations have comparative advantage continues. Robert Baldwin and David Richardson summarized:

> One should not conclude that relative factor proportions are not important in influencing trade patterns, but rather that such productive factors as human capital and natural resources must also be introduced into the traditional model. Furthermore, it is evident that temporary differences in technology, economies of scale, government trade policies, and other factors also play a significant role in determining the commodity structure of world trade. The task now is to ascertain the relative importance of these various elements from country to country and at different times.[10]

CURRENT ANALYSIS OF THE THEORY

The traditional theory of comparative advantage has been challenged because many countries "have indeed succeeded in dramatically altering their comparative advantage."[11] Michael Porter argues that comparative advantage "based on factors of production is not sufficient to explain patterns of trade . . . that the assumptions underlying factor comparative advantage theories of trade are unrealistic in many industries."[12] In today's global economy, a global firm "can locate activities wherever comparative advantage lies, decoupling comparative advantage from the firm's home base. . . . Comparative advantage is specific to the activity and not the location of the value chain as a whole."[13] Each nation or industry starts with certain comparative advantages. These advantages may even sustain for long periods, but they may also frequently shift. A low-labor cost country, for example, can soon be overtaken by another country. An industry "may start with a comparative-advantage-related edge that provides the basis for penetrating foreign markets, but this edge is rapidly translated into a broader array of advantages that arise from the global approach to configuration and coordination."[14] During the last two decades, the factor comparative advantage concept has weakened for three reasons:

1. Technological changes have altered the structure of industries such that the industries today do not resemble the industries on which the traditional model was developed.
2. Comparable factor endowments are now common to many developed nations that account for the bulk of the trade.
3. Globalization of economies have created similar access to resources, technology, and factors of production to international firms.

The nature of international trade "is increasingly being shaped by two competing national strategies, one focused on growth/ productivity and external competitiveness and the other on domestic economic security and redistribution of income."[15] The development strategy is shaped by the country's trade policies, while the distribution strategy allows the forces of free-market to shape economic performance without the intervention of the government.

Thus, Lester Thurow states that in today's global economy "Man-made comparative advantage replaces the comparative advantage of Mother Nature (natural-resources endowments) or history (capital endowments)."[16] Today's international competition between nations, industries, and firms will require continuous creation of new comparative advantages because no advantage can be sustained forever; and no advantage is invincible. The more successful the industry, the more it will be emulated and the more it will be vulnerable to losing its competitive advantage.

American economics is rooted in individualism, while Asian and European economics are based on communitarian values. Those nations are "unwilling to accept comparative advantage as a static notion. . . they are determined to create comparative advantage to suit national goals."[17]

The initial success and growth of Silicon Valley was due to its comparative advantage. Its decline came during the period when it no longer enjoyed those advantages. To regain and retain its competitiveness, it must create new advantages. That may require a fundamental shift in its management ideology, and reevaluating of its economic ideology.

NOTES

1. Harlan Cleveland, *Birth of a New World* (San Francisco: Josey-Bass Publishers, 1993), 143.

2. "Note on Comparative Advantage," *Harvard Business School* (August 1987): 1.

3. Franklin R. Root, *International Trade and Investment* (Cincinnati: South-Western Publishing Co., 1990), 41.

4. "Comparative Advantage," *Harvard Business School*, 1.

5. Peter H. Lindert, *International Economics* (Homewood: Irwin, 1991), 24.

6. Bruce R. Scott and George C. Lodge, *U.S. Competitiveness in the World Economy* (Boston: Harvard Business School Press, 1985), 73.

7. Root, *International Trade and Investment*, 42.

8. "Note on Sources of Comparative Advantage," *Harvard Business School* (April 1989): 1.

9. Ibid., 2.

10. Ibid., 5.

11. Scott, *U.S. Competitiveness*, 75.

12. Michael Porter, *The Competitive Advantage of Nations* (New York: The Free Press, 1990), 12.

13. Michael Porter, ed., *Competing in Global Industries* (Boston: Harvard Business School Press, 1986), 37.

14. Ibid., 38.

15. Scott, *U.S. Competitiveness*, 141.

16. Thurow, *Head to Head*, 16.

17. Lodge, *Perestroika for America*, 17.

Chapter 6

The Growth Analysis

Silicon Valley had unique advantages and characteristics that enabled it to emerge as the leading microelectronics center in the world. This chapter reviews those factors.

SILICON VALLEY BACKGROUND

"Silicon Valley's name has become synonymous with success, growth, and prosperity,"[1] according to Andrew Grove, founder and chief executive officer of Intel Corporation, the largest semiconductor firm in the world.

It is customary for regions, both domestic and foreign, to send delegations to entice local firms to either move, expand or establish operations in their regions. Many regions also endeavor to replicate and imitate the success of Silicon Valley. While this is flattering to Silicon Valley, considering its short history of thirty years, it is also a competitive dilemma.

The term "Silicon Valley" was coined by Don Hoefler in 1971, editor of a weekly scoop sheet for the semiconductor industry. "Silicon" refers to the key ingredient used in the making of a semiconductor chip and the "Valley" refers to the flat landscape of Santa Clara County which is surrounded on the east by the Diablo mountain range and the Santa Cruz mountain range to the west. The term survived. Prior to being named "Silicon Valley," the valley was referred to as "the Prune Capital of America." The agricultural region was the distribution center for agricultural produce from adjacent areas. The electronic revolution during the sixties gradually replaced the orchards and farms with sleek factories, a network of highways, and suburban communities.

Silicon Valley consists of about 1,500 square miles located about fifty miles south of San Francisco with a population of about 1.7 million. According to Tom Forester, author of *High Tech Society*, of the 1,100 firms listed with American Electronics Association, 600 are located in Silicon Valley.[2] By various estimates, Silicon Valley firms, public and private, generate nearly $400 billion in revenues annually, most of it coming from high-technology firms that constitute the "industry of the future."[3] Over 6,000 resident Ph.D.s have contributed to the innovative characteristic of Silicon Valley. The wealth generation capability of Silicon Valley has created over 15,000 millionaires during its history, "making it the greatest concentration of scientific brainpower and new wealth in the USA."[4]

Silicon Valley can be viewed in three different ways, according to Andrew Grove of Intel. Firstly, it is a place, a geographical region of abundant sunshine and excellent climate conditions but also a congested region brought about by its own popularity. Secondly, it is a "business machine" having created over 100,000 manufacturing jobs between 1972 to 1980 and still the world leader in creating new ventures.[5] And finally, it has its own "social characteristics," a unique personality "that distinguishes itself from other regions."[6] A recent Business Week commentary about Silicon Valley stated: "Sure, Silicon Valley has problems-smog, sprawl, and costly labor among them. . . . Despite competition from other would-be high-tech meccas and a growing list of ills, this is still the place where eager entrepreneurs pursue their hearts' desire."[7]

THE GENESIS OF SILICON VALLEY

Arnold Toynbee attributes the rise of a civilization to its ability to respond to challenges. A creative minority responds positively to those challenges in order to generate the growth of a civilization.[8] This phenomenon was evident in Silicon Valley where the challenge was to harness new technologies into creative applications fostering new industries. According to Peter Drucker:[9]

> Innovation is the specific tool of
> entrepreneurs, the means by which they

exploit change as an opportunity for a different business or a different service. It is capable of being presented as a discipline, capable ofbeing learned, capable of being practiced. Entrepreneurs need to search purposefully for the sources ofinnovation, the changes and their symptoms that indicate opportunities for successful innovation. And they need to know and to apply the principles of successful innovation.

The discovery of the transistor was the breakthrough that launched Silicon Valley into singular prominence as the world's largest concentration of innovative industry. This origination led to the creation of the semiconductor, an achievement that enabled millions of electronic circuits to be etched on a quarter square inch silicon wafer. Miniaturization of electronic circuits led to the development of the microprocessor—the brain of the computer—where all the computation took place. A computer-on-a-chip was created. The ability to process millions of algorithms per second was the driving force that would transform the industrial structure by creating new industries. The quintessential technology was now readily available for production.

Perhaps the electronics industry in Silicon Valley would not have emerged without the presence of Stanford University in Palo Alto. Founded in 1885 by Leland Stanford who adopted "the German higher-education model, which stressed research along with teaching."[10] The university's commitment to research enabled it "to attract the world's best scientists."[11]

Each civilization needs a creative minority of people who are able to advance it. William Shockley, one of its most noted professors, invented the "transistor" as part of a research team at Bell Laboratories and consequently won the Nobel Prize in Physics in 1956. He then founded the Shockley's Transistor Lab which produced future Silicon Valley entrepreneurs like Robert Noyce, inventor of the integrated circuit; Gordon Moore, who cofounded Intel Corporation with Noyce and Andy Grove; and Sheldon Roberts, who formed Fairchild Semiconductor, the first semiconductor firm in the Valley. The seeds for the emergence of the new Valley were sown. As an example of resulting prodigious growth, from Fairchild there emerged about 50 spin off companies.

Stanford University continued to play a major role through the leadership of Frederick Terman "who developed Stanford's distinguished Department of Engineering,"[12] and facilitated research in solid-state devices and other technologies that would lay the foundation for the electronics revolution. Terman's philosophy was to form "a symbiotic relationship with industry in which Stanford could serve as the brain trust for new technology-based industries."[13] He founded the Stanford Industrial Park which became a major breeding ground for technical innovators. From this relationship emanated Silicon Valley legends such as David Packard and William Hewlett who founded the multibillion dollar firm Hewlett-Packard, and Russell Varian who founded Varian Associates. Terman's vision and belief that research and development thrives "on a campus-like setting has been embraced by scores of technology firms"[14] and is the trademark of Silicon Valley. In a speech to the graduating class at Dartmouth in 1989, T.J. Rodgers, founder, president and chief executive officer of Cypress Semiconductor Corporation, explained the earlier semiconductor growth revolution:

> Fairchild, of course, became the proverbial mother of Silicon Valley. Virtually every semiconductor company in Silicon Valley spun out of Fairchild. . . . In the late 1960s, there was a tremendous revolution which formed what I call the mega-companies of Silicon Valley—Intel, AMD, and National Semiconductor—which are all now bigger than one billion dollars a year in sales.[15]

The ease of availability of capital to start these new ventures during that time was explained by Andrew Grove:

> "It may be a shock to many people to find this out-but we never wrote a business plan, never wrote a prospectus. We just said we're going into business, would you like to support it?"[16]

Research and development have been a paramount part of the development of Silicon Valley. But the overall success of Silicon Valley is attributed to the early entrepreneurial pioneers who were able to convert the technological developments "to the next steps of application, product development, testing, and eventually marketing by a support system of trained personnel."[17] The achievement and contribution of Silicon Valley to modern society was extolled by *The Economist* in its evaluation of the modern seven wonders of the world. It named the development of the microprocessor by Intel as its number one wonder: "Within the space of a decade it moved from the realm of esoteric high-technology to become a commodity that no modern business could do without. And that is just the start of the microprocessor revolution."[18]

INDUSTRY CHARACTERISTICS

The high-technology electronics industry created by Silicon Valley has unique characteristics that differentiates it from other industries. The author has identified the following key elements:

- An unusually high proportion of highly trained engineers, scientists, professionals and managers, mostly with electronics and computer skills backgrounds. Correspondingly, professionals in the support functions, marketing, customer service, and manufacturing, require advanced technical backgrounds.
- A well-trained and skilled manufacturing work force with comprehensive knowledge of electronic assembly, packaging, and testing.
- An extraordinarily high growth industry, especially during the industry's entrepreneurial and early stages of incubation. Singular management and decision making skills are required in the early stages of the firm's existence according to Larry Griener in his article "Evolution and Revolution as Organizations Grow." The long-term success of the firm depends on its ability to successfully make the evolutionary transitions.[19]
- A high-risk industry characterized by frequent business failures. According to a Santa Clara University study:

> A relatively high 95 percent of Silicon
> Valley start-ups survive the first four years,
> but 25 percent fail to survive their
> "adolescent transition" and collapse in the
> second four years. Of 250 firms founded in
> the 1960s, 31 percent survived, 32 percent
> had been acquired or merged, and 37
> percent had gone bust.[20]

- High research and development expenses in ratio to revenues.
  According to the 1990 data submitted by the Semiconductor
  Industry Association, R&D spending accounted for nearly 12
  percent of firm's annual revenues. This implies "that minimum
  annual sales of $750 million are needed to keep costs competitive
  and carry R&D expenses." [21]
- Development of products that are proprietary and possess short
  product life cycles that force continuous innovation in process
  improvements, for example "consolidation of more functions onto a
  smaller set of chips,"[22] and large investments in plant and
  equipment.
- "A worldwide market for its products,"[23] which is still growing and
  emerging, thus attracting new entrants and creating intense global
  competition.
- Declining production costs by as much as "30 percent for every
  doubling of cumulative volume."[24] Low production costs reduce
  prices, thus decreasing profit margins, which in turn force firms to
  create new products to increase their profit margins in order to
  continue required research and development spending.
- Decidedly limited name brand loyalty, forcing firms to compete on
  price/performance advantage thus intensifying global competition
  and pitting regions against regions to offer tax, capital, and
  property incentives to firms.

The Silicon Valley business culture played a predominant part
in harnessing and exploitingthe characteristics of the industry. In
High-Tech Society, Tom Forester explains:

> Components of this business climate include a good communications infrastructure; ready supplies of venture capital; an abundance of skilled, mobile and mostly nonunion labor; and a high value placed on the individual, entrepreneurship and money-making.[25]

Any given industry and business culture are created by people. The key individuals who pioneered Silicon Valley migrated from the Eastern United States and Europe "to escape the restrictions of hidebound cultures and companies, attracted by the opportunity and openness of California society."[26] A noted Silicon Valley venture capitalist, Don Valentine remarked:

> The East is large companies and rigid structures. The individual doesn't fit well in them. California is the frontier: unstructured economically, socially and institutionally, and above all with a real commitment to personal net worth. That's why Silicon Valley grew up here and not somewhere else.[27]

Silicon Valley's emphasis on individual recognition and achievement encouraged creativity and "a distinct Silicon Valley style of doing business."[28] This style "blended smart management, intensely hard work, and risk taking with it an enlightened attitude toward employees that included egalitarianism and lush benefits."[29] Furthermore, its business culture accepted failures. As Charles O'Reilley, a Berkeley professor noted: "People are encouraged to be creative. And they're not punished for failing."[30] Many entrepreneurs, whose first venture failed, could still obtain venture funding as long as they came up with "the right product, the right management team, and the right marketing concept."[31]

The unique synergy between the individual talent, industry characteristics, fertile University research support, strong educational environment, availability of venture funding, and the Bay Area's attraction created the right ingredients for the emergence of Silicon Valley electronics industry.

ANALYSIS OF THE GROWTH OF SILICON VALLEY

The synergistic characteristics in Silicon Valley that created the microelectronic revolution laid the foundation for its growth. By themselves, innovations do not create businesses or industries. It is the transference of the innovation to products and services that a consumer needs and is willing to purchase. An industry will grow if there is a demand for its products and services. Businesses are created to fulfill consumer demand. As Peter Drucker said: "There is only one valid definition of business purpose: to create a customer. Markets are not created by God, nature, or economic forces but by businessmen."[32] Silicon Valley grew because it was able to transform its innovation into marketable products. Silicon Valley's strength included: "a concentration of technical, marketing, financial, and managerial know-how . . . and rich deposits of brainpower,"[33] the key ingredients for this industry. Timing also played a critical role in the growth of Silicon Valley. The initial Silicon Valley firms blossomed "as the nation's post war economy was booming and the Defense Department was pumping money into the infant electronics industry to create the gadgetry for the cold war."[34]

In *Innovation and Entrepreneur*, Peter Drucker theorizes the relationship between innovation and growth. Industry will grow if innovation exploits change. In some cases, innovation creates change.[35] Silicon Valley flourished because its innovations created change in industry structure and market demands.

Two other theories were advanced to explain the growth of Silicon Valley. The first theory expounded "that small firms are somehow better suited to new high-technology fields than are big ones."[36] The theory is based on George Gilder's "law of the microcosm," which suggests that small entrepreneurial firms have a natural advantage in the new "micro" technologies of the high-tech age."[37] In Gilder's words:

> Rather than pushing decisions up through the hierarchy, microelectronics pulls them remorsely down to the individual. This is the secret of the new American challenge in the global economy and with the microprocessor related chip technologies, the computing industry has replaced its

previous economies of scale with new
economies of microscale.[38]

The second theory advocates "that networks or communities of
small firms are a more effective form of economic and technological
organization than are large integrated companies."[39] The main
proponents of this history, Michael Piore and Charles Sabel, argue
"that 'flexibly specialized' networks of small firms are characterized
by close relationships, shared trust, and intense cooperation in the
development and production of new products."[40] According to this
theory, Silicon Valley constituted "high-technology versions of
"cooperative" industrial districts where firms cooperate with one
another in the development of new products, making it possible for
them to remain small but still be globally competitive."[41] Part of the
success of Silicon Valley can be explained by these theories.

Silicon Valley was founded by entrepreneurs who started new
firms that were different in style than traditional electronic firms.
Small firms led the technology revolution and not the giant firms with
abundant resources, such as General Electric, Texas Instruments,
IBM, Motorola, GTE Sylvania, RCA, and Zenith. It is also true that
many Silicon Valley firms initially cooperated to achieve market
domination. Many of the original entrepreneurs were from the same
institutional and business environment and had a common goal of
creating a new industrial revolution. However, the earlier cooperative
relationships turned into fierce competition as the firms tried to
penetrate new markets and increase market share; and pressure to
create new products intensified.

The United States government initially played an important
role in the growth of the industry in two areas. During the earlier
stages of the industry, the Department of Defense and NASA
accounted for the bulk of the purchases of semiconductors for military
use. Semiconductor firms benefited from providing products to a
captive customer at predetermined prices. Secondly, government
provided research and development funding for private industry in the
form of development contracts and to research laboratories and
institutions for scientific research.

As the semiconductor industry discovered new commercial
applications with broader and wider markets, it began to deemphasize
government sales and sought bigger consumer and industrial markets
worldwide. During the first stage of the industry life cycle, firms

penetrated new markets and the rate of growth was high. Table 6.1 shows the growth of worldwide semiconductor sales from 1959 to 1984.

TABLE 6.1

WORLDWIDE SEMICONDUCTOR SALES ($ BILLIONS)

Year	1959	1964	1969	1974	1979	1984
Sales	0.75	1.25	1.75	5.50	10.75	21.50

Source: Federal State Commission Staff Report, January 77. Business Week, 3 December 1979.

Table 6.2 shows semiconductor sales by end-users between 1960 and 1969. The significance of this chart is the substantially declining trend in shipments to the military and the increase of shipments to consumer and industrial users.

TABLE 6.2

DISTRIBUTION OF U.S. SEMICONDUCTOR SALES BY END USE
(percent)

End Use	1960	1968	1974	1979
Computer	30.0	35.0	28.6	30.0
Consumer	5.0	10.0	23.8	27.5
Military	50.0	35.0	14.3	10.0
Industrial	15.0	20.0	33.3	32.5
Total Value ($ millions)	560	1,211	5,400	10,500

Source: Dataquest.

Table 6.3 shows the number of entrants in the market between 1956 and 1987.

TABLE 6.3

U.S. SEMICONDUCTOR STARTUPS AND CLOSINGS
Number of Firms, 1956-1987

Years	Startups	Closing
1956-1965	10	2
1966-1976	60	20
1977-1987	158	10

Source: Dataquest, 1988.

The new firms entering the market created new applications for their products. Semiconductors and microprocessors offered a variety of applications in different fields: checkout counters, video recorders, automobiles, facsimile machines, telephones, and household appliances; and in different industries: biotechnology, medical equipment, entertainment, and telecommunications. The market potential was virtually unlimited worldwide, especially with no competition to the industry. During the industry's initial stage of growth demand considerably exceeded the supply, and whatever was produced was sold. Because of the excessive demand, the business and industrial system could afford to tolerate inefficiencies and imperfections.

As Silicon Valley firms began to fear domestic market saturation, they focused their marketing effort towards overseas markets. Unrestrained competition developed between local suppliers to capture the growing world market, igniting price wars between themselves. Based on this new development, there were two major competitive options available to local firms.

Firstly, to combat price decreases, Silicon Valley firms established assembly plants in developing countries which lured the firms by offering many low-cost incentives. The long-term impact on the United States economy by the transfer of manufacturing jobs was not fully comprehended by either the industry or the government. American technical knowledge, manufacturing skills, and U.S. capital were being made available to developing countries to cultivate their own economies and industrial infrastructures. Eventually, low-cost foreign products were competing in the American market with those built by American workers.

Secondly, in order to capture the growing world market while limited by their own production capabilities, Silicon Valley firms licensed their technologies to Japanese firms hoping to generate revenues through royalty income. Again, Silicon Valley firms were short-sighted and did not realize that once the Japanese mastered the technology and manufacturing, they would become formidable competitors. During the growth years, Silicon Valley firms were focused on capturing world market share at whatever the cost or the method employed.

The reasons for Silicon Valley's growth during the 1960s and 1970s can be summarized as follows:

1. It created a new industry that engendered new markets.
2. The industry faced minimal worldwide competitive opposition.
3. The large and growing market enabled it to sell anything it produced.
4. Since it was a new industry, it attracted new, and sometimes, naive customers who were fascinated by the new gadgets, products, and technology.
5. The technological advancements it created proliferated new applications in different industries and markets.
6. The industry's growth concealed imperfections and inefficiencies in its organization structures.

In addition, it can be argued that the initial success, growth, and market domination of Silicon Valley was because of the unusual characteristics and young age of the industry rather than creative business endeavors.

The comparative advantage factors during the genesis and growth of Silicon Valley were:

1. Ability to innovate new technologies.
2. Technical expertise in translating new technology developments from basic research to consumer applications.
3. Availability of highly skilled scientists, engineers, researchers, management professionals, and skilled workers.
4. Limited, and in some cases, nonexistent competition.

5. Substantial availability of capital through private venture funding sources eager to participate in the growing and financially rewarding industry.
6. Proximity to outstanding educational and research institutions.
7. Attractive geographical region, excellent year-round warm climate, and casual lifestyle.
8. Supportive local institutional and services infrastructure.

These comparative advantages provided the operating framework for industry leaders to develop business strategies that seemed appropriate during that period. Manybusiness decisions made during that period would later haunt Silicon Valley businesses.

NOTES

1. Andrew Grove, "The Future of Silicon Valley," *California Management Review* (Spring 1987), 154.

2. Tom Forester, *High-Tech Society* (Boston: The MIT Press, 1987), 50.

3. Everett M. Rogers and Judith K. Larsen, *Silicon Valley Fever: Growth of High-Technology Culture* (New York: Basic Books, 1984), 29.

4. Forester, *High-Tech Society*, 51.

5. Grove, *The Future of Silicon Valley*, 154.

6. Ibid., 154.

7.Richard Brandt, "Silicon Valley," *Business Week*, Enterprise 1993, 169.

8. Arnold Toynbee, *A Study of History* (New York: Oxford University Press, 1946).

9. Peter F. Drucker, *Innovation and Entrepreneurship* (New York: Harper Business, 1985), 119.

10. *Silicon Valley: Inventing the Future* (Santa Clara), 107.

11. Ibid., 108.

12. Ibid., 108.

13. Ibid., 108.

14. Ibid., 110.

15. An Address to the Graduating Class at the Investiture of the Dartmouth College: Thayer School of Engineering [10 June 1989].

16. Dirk Hanson, *The New Alchemists: Silicon Valley and the Micro-Electronics Revolution* (New York: Avon Books, 1982), 116.

17. Ibid., 112.

18. *The Economist* (London), 25 December 1993-7 January 1994.

19. Larry E. Griener, "Evolution and Revolution as Organizations Grow," *Harvard Business Review* (July-August 1972), 40-46.

20. Forester, *High-Tech Society*, 57.

21. Peter F. Cowhey and Jonathan D. Aronson, *Managing the World Economy: The Consequences of Corporate Alliances* (New York: Council on Foreign Relations Press, 1993), 129-30.

22. Ibid., 130.
23. Rogers, *Silicon Valley Fever*, 29.
24. "The Global Semiconductor Industry," *Harvard Business School*, March 22, 1993.
25. Forester, *High-Tech Society*, 54.
26. Ibid., 54.
27. Ibid., 54-5.
28. Brandt, "Silicon Valley," *Business Week*, Enterprise 1993, 179.
29. Ibid., 179.
30. Ibid., 179.
31. Ibid., 179.
32. Peter F. Drucker, *The Practice of Management* (New York: Harper & Row, 1954), 37.
33. Brandt, "Silicon Valley," *Business Week*, Enterprise 1993, 170.
34. Ibid., 179.
35. Drucker, *Innovation and Entrepreneurship*, 35.
36. Richard Florida and Martin Kenney, "Silicon Valley and Route 128 Won't Save Us," *California Management Review* (Fall 1990): 68.
37. Ibid., 68-9.
38. Ibid., 69.
39. Ibid., 69.
40. Ibid., 69.
41. Ibid., 69.

Chapter 7

The Shift In Comparative Advantages

> Taking everything into account, [the
> wise prince] will find that some of the
> things that appear to be virtues will, if he
> practices them, ruin him, and some of the
> things that appear to be vices will bring
> him security and prosperity.

> *Niccolo Machiavelli*
> The Prince

Silicon Valley is competing in a very different global
environment than the one in which it proliferated. The comparative
advantage it once enjoyed does not exist anymore. Many other regions
of the world have replicated the advantages and fiercely compete
against Silicon Valley firms in all markets. The unique combination of
talent, capital, and infrastructure propelled Silicon Valley to
domination of the world microelectronic industry. Although the same
synergistic ingredients still existed, the Valley declined in
competitiveness and suffered a considerable loss of market share.

There has been a paradigm shift of comparative advantage
factors from Silicon Valley to other regions of the world. Five
reasons that have caused the shift in advantages can be delineated.
Three are internal to Silicon Valley and relate to the behavior of the
firms and the industry; and two are external to Silicon Valley, caused
by the change in the nature of economic competition and the roles
foreign government and industries have played in creating new
comparative advantages. While all five reasons created a shift of

comparative advantage from Silicon Valley to other regions, the role of government is the most significant. A study by Semiconductor Industry Association concluded:

> Government policies have shaped the course of international competition in microelectronics virtually from the inception of the industry, producing outcomes completely different than would have occurred through the operation of the market alone.[1]

The paradigm shift in advantage was caused by the following factors:

1. Business strategies of Silicon Valley firms during growth period.
2. Industry fragmentation.
3. Inconsistent industry/government relationship.
4. Changing nature of global competition.
5. Comparative advantages created abroad.

This chapter analyzes the first three factors.

BUSINESS STRATEGIES OF SILICON VALLEY FIRMS

"Firms, not nations, compete in international markets,"[2] according to Michael Porter. Firms compete within the industry and in global markets through competitive advantage positioning. The two types of competitive advantage are: lower cost and differentiation. Lower cost derives from a firm's ability "to design, produce, and market a comparable product more efficiently than its competitors,"[3] while differentiation implies the firm's ability "to provide unique and superior value to the buyer."[4]

Firms create cost and differentiation advantage in global markets through dispersing activities among several nations to improve market access and logistics; locating activities in other regions to gain economic and specialization advantage; and, through global coordination and alliances which will achieve access to foreign markets, obtain necessary technology, spread risk, and shape industry structure. Most Silicon Valley firms followed the Michael Porter model of competitive strategy.

To accommodate the growing worldwide demand for its products, Silicon Valley firms adopted business strategies that, on the surface, seemed appropriate for the market conditions at that time. Competition was intensifying in domestic markets and local firms did not have the production capacity to meet the growing worldwide demand for their products. To create low cost advantage and increase foreign market penetration, Silicon Valley firms basically pursued two generic strategies:

1. Establishing overseas manufacturing operations at low-labor cost regions to obtain the cost advantage which made their products price competitive and increased market share.
2. Licensing technology and manufacturing rights to overseas firms, especially Japanese firms, to gain access to capital and markets.

By adopting these strategies, Silicon Valley firms were shifting comparative advantages to firms in other countries. Lenny Siegel of Pacific Studies Center remarked: "As long as U.S. companies have been manufacturing integrated circuits, they have assembled those chips overseas . . . the economic patriotism of the owners is suspect."[5]

Although licensing technology does provide short-term access to foreign markets, the long-term repercussions of licensing are serious. Michael Porter identifies two major problems. Firstly, it creates future competitors, and secondly, it gives away the firm's competitive advantage for a meager royalty fee. It "is an easy way of increasing short-term profits, but it can result in a long-term erosion in profits as a firm's competitive advantage dissipates."[6]

Silicon Valley business strategies provided other countries with easy access to new technology and manufacturing know-how at a fraction of what it would have cost them to develop on their own. Many developing countries, such as Singapore, Taiwan, South Korea, encouraged this opportunity to invigorate their developing economies, increase their standard of living, and develop a skilled work force.

Silicon Valley firms had, in effect, started the process of transference of comparative advantage.

INDUSTRY FRAGMENTATION

As the microelectronic market grew, cracks began to appear within the industry. To capitalize on the mushrooming market, the industry experienced a "proliferation of 'me-too startups,' or copy cat companies. Me-too start-ups are linked to 'technology fads.'"[7] Don Valentine, a venture capitalist, explained: "The sopping up of resources by multiple startups . . . is detracting from the competitiveness of U.S. resources."[8] The result was a major shake-out in the industry creating "large financial losses and massive layoffs."[9]

The industry is both horizontally and vertically fragmented. Horizontal fragmentation splits the business into various core businesses, thus forcing many firms to rely on a single core product. The industry can be fragmented into integrated circuit producers, subcontract manufacturers, computer manufacturers, design specialists, equipment manufacturers, and hardware producers. Unlike the Japanese firms, this narrow product base makes it "impossible to cross-subsidize products, leaving firms vulnerable to major technological changes, price swings, and industry downturns."[10] A slump in one segment affects other segments. For example, computer sales declines hurt semiconductor sales; and the involved highly specialized firms are vulnerable to international competition and price wars.

Vertical fragmentation means that various functions of the organization are decentralized or located in other regions. This fragmentation makes it difficult for firms to coordinate their design and manufacturing efforts. The design function in Santa Clara may never have seen the manufacturing operations in Singapore.

According to the California Management Review article on Silicon Valley:

> The highly fragmented structure of U.S. microelectronics has created patterns and rules of behavior that make it extremely difficult for companies to integrate. . . . while U.S. semiconductor

and computer firms are engaged in this
frantic jockeying for position, large
integrated Japanese corporations continue to
make greater and greater inroads in
virtually every microelectronic market from
mass-produced semiconductors to custom
chips and from laptops and personal
computers to high-end supercomputers.[11]

Such fragmentation has hurt the industry's ability to compete.
Japanese firms take advantage of this fragmentation and fashion
strategic alliances with many of these specialized firms. The study
concludes:

The fragmentation and splintering of
our high-technology capabilities makes it
ever more difficult to build stable
companies and industries that can compete
over the long haul. . . . the extreme
segmentation of the high-technology
production process drastically inhibits
technological follow-through and hinders
American industry's ability to meet the
challenge of emerging global competition.[12]

In an article, AnnLee Saxenian identifies one of the key
ingredients to success of Silicon Valley as "collective learning as new
ideas are continually recombined with existing skill, technology,
know-how, and experience."[13] This innovative network of
entrepreneurs, technologists, and financial supporters shattered as
firms began to compete on commodity products. Price sensitivity and
market share control became the dominant competitive elements. Price
and cost factor pressures of commodity production forced Silicon
Valley firms to shift manufacturing out of the region to lower cost
locations. "This spatial separation of design, manufacturing, and
assembly further undermined the ability of local semiconductor firms
to improve products or to respond rapidly to market changes."[14] Ms.
Saxenian summed up the impact of this trend on Silicon Valley:

By adopting an autarkic version of
mass production just as the Japanese were
refining a highly integrated approach
however, Silicon Valley's merchant
producers fell behind in customer relations,
manufacturing improvements and product
quality and quickly lost market share to
Japanese competitors.[15]

INCONSISTENT INDUSTRY/GOVERNMENT RELATIONSHIP

The industry and government relationship has been anything
but planned, cooperative, and coordinated. It fluctuated, depending on
the economic and market conditions of the period. There have been
four distinct phases in this relationship since the inception of the
industry.

The first phase started at the emergence of the industry and
lasted through the early 1960s. During this phase, there was extensive
interaction between government agencies, particularly the Department
of Defense and NASA, and firms in the industry. "This interaction
arose from the government's great interest in military and space
applications of semiconductor technology and its willingness to fund
company R&D directed toward more reliable devices."[16] Government
was a major captive buyer of semiconductors from local firms.

The second phase continued through the 1960s and "may be
described as one of laissez faire."[17] During this phase the government
demand decreased rapidly, consequently new commercial applications
were discovered "that were more attractive to many of the firms in the
industry."[18] The government and industry relationship dwindled to a
customer/supplier relationship, and no new operational policy was
adopted or implemented.

The third phase during the 1970s can be categorized as "one of
increased frustration by industry executives with government
policy."[19] As the industry faced foreign competition, elevated by the
support foreign governments provided for their own manufacturers, it
found the Americangovernment tax and trade policies inadequate and
unsupportive for equitable competition in the world market. The

"once cordial relationship"[20] between government and industry became adversarial.

The fourth phase emerged in the 1980s and can be categorized as one of attempting to build a lasting and economically productive relationship. The forced marriage between government and industry is forged by common economic interests. During the 1980s, Silicon Valley firms' loss of considerable market share to foreign firms also impacted the U.S. economy.

Throughout the history of the microelectronics industry, the government and industry relationship has been driven by selfish and short-term economic interests. The industry and government relationship remains cordial but uncoordinated and inconsistent. One of the major reasons for the inability of the government and industry to work together to form a long-term economic development policy that will benefit both industry and the U.S. economy lies in the American ideology that promulgates free-market competition without government interference.

Cooperation between industry and government is all the more necessary in view of the competition in global markets where foreign industry and government are collaborating to achieve economic prosperity. In this connection, the *San Jose Mercury News* carried an important headline in its business section in November 1992, which stated: "Globalization of technology muddles policy," and commented on the continuing lack of government technology policy in support of the industry. As technologies are easily traded across national boundaries, government policies that do not adapt to this fundamental industrial shift invite failure.

Further, within the microelectronic industry there is a divergence of views on the major issues that confront the industry. This lack of unification continues to deter the development of a uniform industrial policy with the government. The key issues are: trading, intellectual property, and research and development investment.

Trading

Trading encompasses tariffs, protectionism, export controls, and dumping issues. Tariffs are taxes or duties imposed by the government to control the flow of imported goods into the country. By applying tariffs the government increases the price of an imported product, thus reducing its demand. Because the governments of many nations have developed such tariff policies, in the United States the electronics industry has lobbied for tariffs and quotas to protect its markets. The industry has also approached the government to pressure other governments, especially Japan, to open their markets to American semiconductor and computer products. Recent lobbying efforts by semiconductor firms pressured the American government to negotiate semiconductor import and export quotas from Japan.

The ideological policy disagreement between industry and government officials was debated in a *San Francisco Chronicle* article regarding a meeting between Silicon Valley officials and Carla Hills, the U.S. Trade Representative in 1992 which stated that "she disliked 'managed trade'"[21] and imposing ceilings may hurt U.S. firms. Simultaneously, an industry spokesman commented: "Rather than making excuses for why Japan is not meeting its commitments under the agreement, the U.S. trade representative should be pounding the table getting Japan to open up its market."[22]

While tariffs have existed for many years, the issue of tariffs is relatively new for Silicon Valley. Technology firms feel that the government imposes such tariffs without regard to overall economic conditions or competitive considerations.

A recent case concerning the complaint by computer manufacturers substantiates this contention. The dispute concerns import of flat-panel screens and displays used in laptop and notebook computers. Japanese manufacturers perfected this technology before American firms and placed it in production far in advance of American manufacturers. An Oregon company, Planar Corporation, manufacturing flat screens for the Department of Defense, complained to the Department of Commerce that Japanese firms were selling their product in the United States below cost, also referred to as dumping, thus making it difficult for Planar to compete and sell its product to American firms. Planar had no record of producing this product commercially.

Hearings were held in Washington D.C. where American computer companies testified that they needed the Japanese product from Japan to compete in the global market. In July 1991, the U.S. Commerce Department ruled that Japanese manufacturers of the flat-panel screens were dumping the product in the United States. The International Trade Commission then imposed a 62.67 percent tariff on the Japanese screens "to protect the tiny, struggling U.S.

flat-screen industry."[23] This was opposed by computer firms who saw this tariff increasing their product costs, thereby making it expensive in international markets where they were competing against Japanese and European firms. To avoid paying this tariff, American computer manufacturers moved analogous computer manufacturing outside the United States. *The New Republic* commented:

> The flat-panel decision is a disaster for American competitiveness. It has penalized American computer makers because it adds more than $1,100 to the cost of producing each laptop, an expense that their foreign competitors will not have to contend with. U.S. companies are nowhere nearer to producing flat panels. And thousands of American jobs have moved overseas.[24]

In September 1991, Toshiba announced that it was shifting its American-based production of laptops back to Japan, costing additional American jobs. In December 1991, computer firms filed complaints petitioning the Court of International Trade to reverse the tariff decision.

On June 21, 1993, the Commerce Department reversed itself and revoked the 63 percent tariff it had imposed on flat-panel screens from Japan nearly two years previously. During those two years, not only did American firms lose market share on laptops, but lost jobs to overseas manufacturing plants as well. Industry specialists stated: "This was done with no clear policy direction. . . . Somebody's going to have to take responsibility if we are going to get a comprehensive approach."[25]

The flat-panel display issue did not subside. After American firms lost the market to Japanese firms and moved assembly of laptop computers overseas, the United States government announced that it would spend "$300 million or so over the next five years as part of the federal government's ongoing efforts to create, nearly from scratch, a domestic flat-panel display industry."[26] The rationale behind the government move is to support the requirements for military applications since the Japanese firm Sharp Corporation, which dominates the flat-screen market, "refuses to sell directly to the U.S. military or provide it with early versions of its products, which the military needs for a host of systems."[27] Silicon Valley firms welcomed the government's actions as they would benefit from this funding. However, if the United States government had responded to the Japanese flat-panel threat five years ago, the American firms today would not have to start from scratch in creating this new emerging industry. Ironically, the Department of Commerce reversed themselves two years later and removed the tariffs. The damage was done. American workers lost jobs and high-technology firms had to spend substantial resources in arguing with the U.S. government. There was no working relationship and everyone lost.

Protectionism

Protectionist policy involves creating government rules and guidelines that improve the competitive situation of the industry. Protectionism is contrary to the free-market ideology of American institutions. Major conflict disagreement exists on this issue within the microelectronics industry.

Generally, a particular segment of the industry solicits protectionist policy from the government when facing stiff or unfair international competition or more often, when experiencing competitiveness decline. Semiconductor firms sought U.S. government intervention only when their market shares dwindled. "Despite Silicon Valley's well-deserved reputation for individualism,"[28] it did not hesitate to lobby the government for protectionist policies against Japanese firms. However, local software and work station manufacturers such as Sun Microsystems and Hewlett-Packard, who dominate their markets, do not want U.S. government protectionist policies for fear of international retaliation of their dominance.

Since there is no uniform consensus, it becomes difficult to develop a uniform trade policy. The American issue-oriented system focuses on the predilections of the winners and losers in the industry. Export control policies follow a similar pattern.

Export Controls

Export controls against Silicon Valley were initiated by the United States government to protect the defense industry and prevent the sale "of strategically important"[29] high-technology products to certain nations, particularly the Soviet Union, People's Republic of China, and Eastern bloc countries. The export control policy was established in 1949 by the U.S. government during the creation of the NATO alliance. Although the Cold War ended, government policy changed little. When the Silicon Valley emerged as the center for high-technology, it was subject to the same control procedures that were brought into being more than three decades earlier.

Forbes magazine's article in April 1990 commented: "Technology is slamming right into the regulatory machinery. U.S. high-tech firms suffer from outdated export controls."[30]

This led high-technology companies to argue that "the need for export licenses involves red tape that slows their competitive responses; Pentagon and State Department objections often cost them orders around the world."[31] Since the technology is readily available worldwide, firms in other nations have an advantage in capturing the world market. According to the *Forbes* article, this export control could "cripple a most promising $5 billion to $10 billion high-performance computer industry."[32] Furthermore, in order to meet the export requirements, the firms "may be forced to underdesign their products."[33]

As late as 1990, personal computers utilizing Intel 16-bit computers were barred from overseas sales to certain countries without special licensing. Also still barred are technical work stations manufactured by the Silicon Valley firms: Sun Microsystems and Hewlett-Packard. However, comparable work stations are presently available through Japanese and European manufacturers who do not encounter government restrictions. A recent study by the Institute of International Economics concluded "that U.S. export controls, licensing procedures, embargoes and regulations cost the United States anywhere from $25 billion to $40 billion a year in overseas sales."[34] In contrast, Japan's trade barrier against American goods amount to only "$9 billion to $18 billion annually."[35]

Dumping

Silicon Valley has often claimed that foreign firms, especially Japanese and other Asian firms, increase their market share in the United States by "dumping" their products. Dumping is characterized as charging a lower price for a product in an export market than in the home market, or as generally characterized, selling a product for less than the cost of its production. In any case, it represents an unfair competitive practice to the American government. The U.S. Department of Commerce establishes the criteria for evaluating dumping. Robert Reich, author of his bestseller, *The Work of Nations* noted:

> The Commerce Department insists that the foreign company must earn a profit of at least 8 percent. If the foreign company earns anything less than this, the Commerce Department assumes that it is selling the product at a loss, and thus illegally "dumping" it in the United States.[36]

This arbitrary manner of establishing the level of profits firms must make converts the "dumping" issue into a "protectionist" issue.

A *New Republic* article evaluating dumping laws declared that "the anti-dumping law has increasingly been wielded as a protectionist tool. . . . subverting American competitiveness while enriching a handful of industrial laggards."[37] Since 1980 the Commerce Department has found dumping in 95 percent of the cases it examined, using criteria "that hold foreign competitors to absurd standards." Although the average American corporate profit is only 5 to 6 percent, if the foreign firm makes less than 8 percent profit, the Commerce Department can penalize it for dumping.

It is obvious that the law is used effectively by weak high-technology firms to fortify their markets. Earlier discussion of Planar Corporation's flat-panel issue supports this contention.

Intellectual Property

The high-technology industry thrives on innovation and creativity. The United States has led the world in patenting new inventions and technologies. Silicon Valley is a leader in the creation and metamorphosis of new technologies. Unfortunately, a high-technology company cannot rely on patents alone to keep competitors out of a market; especially when outdated U.S. patent laws are applied in the global economy. Section 101 of the U.S. Patent Act states: "Whoever invents or discovers any new and useful process, machine manufacture, or composition of matter, or any new and useful improvement thereof, may obtain a patent therefore, subject to the conditions and requirements of this title." The infringement of the patent law, which was developed for domestic control, is very difficult to enforce in the international market. The technology companies in Silicon Valley face exactly that problem.

Following is a case in point. In 1986, a semiconductor firm filed a patent infringement lawsuit against one Korean and eight Japanese semiconductor firms for producing and selling DRAM memory chips in the United States without having a license. It also filed a complaint against the same foreign firms with the International Trade Commission, using Section 337 of the Tariff Act of 1930. The litigation became a test case for the industry.

Section 337 of the Tariff Act of 1930 authorizes the International Trade Commission to exclude unfairly traded articles from the United States. While this Tariff Act may stop the selling of products in the United States, it does not stop the foreign companies from selling their products in other parts of the world and that is exactly what happened. As the United States appealed to the GATT resolution panel, the panel ruled that Section 337 is inconsistent with the GATT rules and should be changed. It further ruled that the United States applies this section in a more unfavorable manner to products from foreign companies than it does to domestic suppliers. The panel identified six problems with Section 337.

1. Foreign complainants and American complainants have different forums for appeal, which favors the American companies.
2. Time limits are inconsistent for domestic and foreign complainants.
3. Counterclaims are not available under Section 337.
4. There is no court remedy to the general exclusion order as provided to the domestic complainants.
5. Section 337 orders are automatically enforced by the government agency without appeal.
6. Section 337 treats foreign firms differently than domestic firms with the same type of problem.

The United States government complained that GATT "misapplied" the "law" of the GATT, but would review Section 337. Since the administration and Congress differ on the enforcement of this section, there seems to be very little hope that a consensus will emerge on this Section in the near future.

In the meantime, the Silicon Valley firms lost the DRAM market to the Japanese. The loss of this important product to Japanese and Korean firms is attributed to the lack of cooperation between the industry and the government. Outdated American trade laws do not protect or enhance the industry in the international arena where the United States is no longer a dominant economic force.

Research and Development

Silicon Valley declares that research and development is "the lifeblood of their companies."[38] At Hewlett-Packard, products conceived during the last three years account for half its revenues. Yet the growth of R&D spending has dropped off during the last decade. R&D expenditures have to be expensed according to United States government tax rules, therefore the overall profit of the company is reduced. Because the companies are forced to show short-term profits by the shareholders who demand a high rate of return on their investment and managers who command substantial profit-oriented bonuses, the firms have reduced research investment. R&D expenditure entails a long-term risky investment. In many countries, like Germany and Japan, the government shares this risk. Government participation is needed for the overall growth of the nation's economy, and government intervention can support the individual business efforts to pursue R&D activities. Japan's Ministry of International Trade and Industry actively participates with the industry in speculative R&D ventures. No such agency exists in United States.

R&D tax issues also do not favor the high-technology industry. In 1981, Congress allowed limited tax credits for R&D. Initially projected for five years, Congress extends the tax credit policy on an annual basis. Thus, the industry has no horizon for long-term planning. In concept, both the industry and government agree on R&D. President Bush, in his "Building a Better America" message in February 1989, said, "Technology innovation, particularly through U.S.-based research, is essential to maintain our competitive position in the world economy. The controversy concerning the allocation of R&D expense is now well into its second decade. The uncertainty generated by the continued expiration of temporary rules has made for an unstable tax environment for domestic research activity."[39] The government study concluded:

> Research and development is the driving force behind innovation, which enhances the United States' position in the world marketplace and increases American productivity. Therefore, it is difficult to understand why the U.S. government would formulate policies that discourage the pursuit of domestic R&D.[40]

The Internal Revenue Service Regulation 1.861-8 does exactly that. It enforces a penalty tax on American R&D. In its analysis of this regulation, The Council on Research and Technology, concluded:

> Over the last decade, Congress has repeatedly adopted temporary moratoriums to prevent the implementation of the 861 regulations, but has never reached a permanent solution to the 861 problem. This lack of stability makes it difficult, if not impossible, for U.S. industry to implement long-range R&D plans.[41]

The industry and government relationship in this regard has hurt Silicon Valley's competitive position. The resulting weakness has been exploited by Japanese and other Asian nations to make inroads into American and foreign markets. While the United States continues to debate "the stark choice between free markets and state control,"[42] foreign countries continue economic gains through state involved industrial development. "The best economic outcomes seem to be the product of mixed systems,"[43] according to Harlan Cleveland. To compete in tomorrow's economy, Silicon Valley and government will need to consistently cooperate if Silicon Valley is to create new competitive advantages and regain its market dominance.

NOTES

1. James Fallows, "Looking At The Sun," *The Atlantic Monthly*, November 1993, 90.

2. Michael Porter, *The Competitive Advantage of Nations* (New York: The Free Press, 1990), 33.

3. Ibid., 37.

4. Ibid., 37.

5. Lenny Siegel, "Target Real Enemy of Trade," *San Jose Mercury News*, 1993.

6. Michael Porter, *Competitive Advantage: Creating and Sustaining Superior Performance* (New York: The Free Press, 1985), 193.

7. Richard Florida and Martin Kenney, "Silicon Valley and Route 128 Won't Save Us," *California Management Review* (Fall 1990), 74.

8. Ibid., 74.

9. Ibid., 74.

10. Ibid., 76.

11. Ibid., 79.

12. Ibid., 79.

13. AnnaLee Saxenian, "Regional Networks and the Resurgence of Silicon Valley," *California Management Review* (Fall 1990), 98.

14. Ibid., 99.

15. Ibid., 100.

16. Robert W. Wilson, Peter K. Ashton, and Thomas P. Egan, *Innovation, Competition, and Government Policy in the Semiconductor Industry* (Lexington: Lexington Books, 1980), 2.

17. Ibid., 2.

18. Ibid., 2.

19. Ibid., 2.

20. Ibid., 2.

21. John Eckhouse, "Carla Hills Rattles Chip Firms," *San Francisco Chronicle*, 1 February 1992, B1.

22. Ibid., B3.

23. *San Jose Mercury News*, 1992, C1.

24. James Bovard, "Toxic Dumping," *The New Republic*, 9 December 1991, 18.

25. Douglas Harbrecht and Paul Magnusson, "Did Commerce Pull the Plug on Flat-Screen Makers," *Business Week*, 5 July 1993, 32.
26. Lee Gomes, "White House promises another $300 million for flat panels," *San Jose Mercury News*, 29 April 1994, E1.
27. Bob Davis and G. Pascal Zachary, "Electronic Firms Get Push From Clinton to Join Industrial Policy Initiative in Flat-Panel Displays," *The Wall Street Journal*, 28 April 1994, A16.
28. James J. Mitchell, "Alliances make individualistic firms stronger," *San Jose Mercury News*, 17 October 1993.
29. Eduardo Lachica, "U.S. Removes Licensing Rules On Export of High-Tech Products," *The Wall Street Journal*, 13 July 1989, 1.
30. *Forbes*, 16 April 1990, 1.
31. Ibid., 1.
32. Ibid., 1.
33. Ibid., 1.
34. Jonathan Marshall, "Trade Barriers Blamed on U.S.," *San Francisco Chronicle*, February 1994, E1.
35. Ibid., E1.
36. Robert B. Reich, *The Work of Nations: Preparing Ourselves for 21st Century Capitalism* (New York: Alfred A. Knopf, 1991), 71.
37. *The New Republic*, 9 December 1991, 18.
38. Timothy Taylor, "The ominous sputter of R&D," *San Jose Mercury News*, 26 March 1989.
39. Council on Research and Technology, "*Section 861's Disincentive to Domestic R&D*," 1.
40. Ibid., 1.
41. Ibid., 2.
42. Fallows, *The Atlantic Monthly*, November 1993, 100.
43. Harlan Cleveland, *Birth of a New World* (San Francisco: Josey-Bass Publishers, 1993), 142.

Chapter 8

Creating Comparative Advantages Abroad

This chapter analyzes the external factors that led to the shifting of comparative advantages from the Silicon Valley to other regions outside the United States.

THE CHANGING NATURE OF GLOBAL COMPETITION

Firms today compete in global markets. Firms shape global competition. Global competition is very much different today than that in which Silicon Valley evolved. In the 1960s, Silicon Valley firms, competing against a limited number of domestic suppliers, concentrated on fulfilling the domestic demand for its products. During the 1970s, Silicon Valley firms penetrating international markets by exporting products primarily manufactured in their American plants. It enjoyed a competitive advantage through the absence of any foreign major competitors. To satisfy the increased foreign demand and develop price/cost advantage, Silicon Valley firms expanded operations overseas. Foreign firms intensified competition during the 1980s and attacked Silicon Valley firms in both American and foreign markets. The foreign firms were well-financed, well-supported by their governments and financial institutions, and staffed by talented professionals and a skilled work force.

However, there was one major difference. Initially, Silicon Valley firms evolved to compete domestically, while foreign firms evolved to compete globally.

As the nature of competition changed, Silicon Valley's ability to respond to these changes also should have changed. One of the reasons for its loss of competitive advantage was its inability to compete globally in a fiercely competitive environment.

The paradigm shift in global markets eroded the differences of what is actually made and produced in each country. An assembled product today may consist of components and materials engendered in different regions of the world, making it difficult to identify what is "made in America" anymore. Business competition in today's global environment requires different concepts and managerial techniques. Unfortunately, while the nature of competition changed, Silicon Valley firms employed business strategies that were developed by American firms in the 1950s and 1960s when the United States was the dominant economic power and faced insignificant domestic and foreign competition.

Silicon Valley began operating in a global environment during the 1970s. In the 1980s, not only were the Valley manufacturers dependent on other firms in different parts of the world for services and materials, but they needed to provide their own products and services globally. Even in domestic markets, they faced fierce foreign competition.

The firms that were successful in global competition were the ones that were able to move from a multinational operating environment to a global operating environment. Japanese firms had the competitive advantage, because they chose to evolve to compete in U.S. and international markets. Silicon Valley firms had to play a catch-up game of converting from domestic organizations to global competitors.

The difference between a multinational corporation and a global corporation, and the respective abilities of each type of firm to compete in new global competitive environment, can be examined.

Michael Porter, discussing international industrial competitive forces ten years ago, argued:

> To succeed, an international company
> may have to change from a multidomestic
> company, which allows individual
> subsidiaries to compete independently in
> different domestic markets, to a global
> organization which pits its entire worldwide

system of product and market position
against the competition.[1]

Theodore Levitt, discussing the globalization of markets one year
later, predicted the end of the multinational corporation and the birth
of the global corporation.[2]

International considerations have become more important as
international trade has increased. From 1960 through 1986, the
volume of goods traded between all nations has increased from less
than $100 million to $2 trillion annually. American exports, during
the same time period, increased from $20.6 billion to $217 billion (a
three-fold increase in constant dollars) and American imports
increased from $16.4 billion to $387.1 billion (a five-fold increase in
constant dollars).[3] Almost one-fifth of American industrial production
is now exported and approximately 75% of goods produced in the
U.S. compete with products from other countries.[4]

Levitt, in the 1980s, stated that "technology was the driving
force toward a converging commonality that proletarized
communications, transportation, and travel."[5] "Almost everyone,"
Levitt argued, "wants all the things they have heard about, seen or
experienced, via new technologies."[6]

Levitt's views of technology as a conversion force are more
telling today than they were ten years ago. The revolution in
communist countries supports the concept that if people are exposed
to a system, products, and services that meets their needs, they will
gravitate towards it. This concept is brought to the marketplace when
as Levitt states "all people want products that reduce their burden and
improve their standard of living."[7] The combination of technology,
which increases awareness, and people's common desire, creates the
global market for goods.

Many business experts in the 1980s argued that certain
industries would remain multidomestic or multinational and were not
subject to globalization because they were culture-bound and differed
greatly among country markets. These products and industries were
specialized for certain regional markets. Therefore culture-bound
products were primarily used in domestic markets. Other experts
argued against the globalization of certain industries, stating that
products may not achieve proper economies of scale, carry high
transportation costs, create distribution problems, increase service and
support activities, and encounter government barriers.

Levitt, in response to these arguments, states that lack of global imagination and poor execution is a more important cause of failure of globalized products than failure to accommodate to local market preferences.[8] Levitt contends that people will prefer global standardized products that are superior in quality and are cheaper than culture-bound products.[9]

Porter, arguing against the hypothesis that certain products are not conducive to globalization, states that a "large group of international companies have global potential even though they may not know it and that almost every industry that is now global was not at one time."[10] Companies today, with the help of technology, are following Levitt's advice and are seeking to standardize their offerings everywhere and will digress from standardization only after exhausting all possibilities to retain it and will push for reinstatement of standardization whenever divergence has occurred.[11]

Traditionally, corporations expand their operations internationally to increase sales and profits by: increasing market outlets, reducing costs by placing production facilities in locations close to sources of needed raw materials and/or cheap labor, and securing raw material resources.

Many Silicon Valley firms followed the above traditional concept global competition. From the onset, Silicon Valley firms focused on supplying products to international markets, not creating products for the international markets. Their concepts were rooted in the multinational attitude of being a supplier to foreign markets. The global corporation operates "as if the entire world were a single entity."[12] For example, Apple Computers introduced its Macintosh computers in Japan without a manual in Japanese, assuming that Japanese consumer would be able to use the manual written in English. Hamel and Prahalad argue that many firms rationalized their global competitive ability on the basis of operating low-cost manufacturing plants in foreign locations.[13] "Buoyed by these kinds of global strategies, companies firmly believe that they have met the Japanese challenge head on."[14] All these firms did was to produce a low-cost product that could be matched by any other global firm.

Global competition today requires a strategy of cross-subsidization which presupposes that a firm will use all its resources "accumulated in one part of the world to fight a competitive battle in another."[15] Silicon Valley firms did not adopt any such competitive strategies during the 1980s, while the Japanese firms did. Silicon

Valley firms were still fighting international battles using marketing techniques learned during American economic domination.

The growth of globalized competition has allowed an ever-increasing number of companies, which have pursued a global-versus-multidomestic strategy over the past ten years, to gain dominant market positions in their respective industries. Porter, ten years ago, described the basic concepts underlying global corporations, as their use of the "entire worldwide system of product and market positions against another."[16] Porter further notes that in a global corporation "various countries' subsidiaries are highly interdependent in terms of operations and strategies. A country subsidiary may specialize in manufacturing only part of its product line, exchanging products with others in the system. Country profit targets vary, depending upon the individual impact on the cost position or effectiveness of the entire worldwide system. Prices may be set in one country to have an intended end effect in another country. Strategy is centralized and various aspects of operations are centralized as economic and effectiveness dictate. The company seeks to respond to particular local market needs while avoiding a compromise of efficiency of the overall global system."[17]

In contrast, the multidomestic company, Porter states, "pursued separate strategies in each of its foreign markets while viewing the competitive challenges independently from market to market. Each overseas subsidiary is strategically independent with essentially autonomous operations. The multinational headquarters will coordinate financial controls and marketing policies worldwide and may centralize research and development and component production, but strategy and operations are decentralized with each subsidiary a profit center and expected to contribute earnings and growth commensurate with market opportunity."[18] Porter further notes that "in a multi-domestic corporation, a company's management tries to operate effectively across a series of worldwide positions with diverse product requirements, growth rates, competitive environments, and political risk. The company competes with other multi-nationals and local competitors on a market-by-market basis."[19]

According to Peter Drucker, the nature of competition also changed from "competitive trade" to "adversarial trade."[20] "Competitive trade aims at creating a customer," while "adversarial trade aims at dominating an industry."[21] Silicon Valley firms were practicing competitive trade in creating world markets for its products and worrying about market share gains. Japanese firms were aiming at dominating the industry in the long-term through developing competitive advantages. The two competitive business strategies are at odds with each other, and in this case the adversarial strategy prevailed.

The corporation model that was best suited to compete in the 1980s was different from that of the 1960s and 1970s. Silicon Valley firms were competing using outdated management models. They acceded the management competitive advantage to foreign firms.

CREATING COMPARATIVE ADVANTAGES ABROAD

The biggest threat to Silicon Valley's domination in microelectronics came from nations and firms in those nations that combined their efforts and strategies to create comparative advantages that enabled them to compete and, in some cases, dominate some segments of this new industry. Since the microelectronics industry emerged as the foundation for the information industry of the future, it received predominant attention from businesses and governments. Success in this industry would imply economic success in the future. The reason why this factor is important for careful evaluation is that it is based on the ideological preferences of nations which substantially differ from the American ideology. The different ideologies and the history behind the development of those ideologies are identified and discussed in previous chapters.

Another reason for the significance of this factor is that it involves a planned coordinated effort on the part of government and businesses to dominate certain industries. It is generally assumed that capitalistic free-market competition is determined by the demand and supply forces in the economy. Actually, the success and failure of a firm is tied to its economic ability to compete in the marketplace. Government's role is seen as that of a provider of public and social infrastructure to promote free-market competition, not as an active economic partner determining the direction of the industry and firms. Government intervention is seen as impinging on the forces of demand and supply. Therein lies the difference between American and Japanese capitalist systems. The American economic system abhors government intervention, while the Japanese economic system welcomes government intervention.

The American economic model is based on the economic principles of Adam Smith in *The Wealth of Nations* in 1776. Simply stated, Adam Smith's argument is: "If each individual pursues his own self-interest, an invisible hand will automatically serve the common interests of the larger society. So, social goals are a by-product of self-interest."[22] In Adam Smith's words:

> Every individual . . . intends only his own gain, and he is in this, as in many other cases, led by an invisible hand to promote an end which was no part of his intention. . . . by pursuing his own self interest he frequently promotes that of the society more effectively than when he really intends to promote it. I have never known much good done by those who affected to trade for the public good.

Contrary to conventional American thinking, the Japanese and German capitalism model is not based on the economic principles of Adam Smith. The credit goes to an obscure German economist, Friedrich List, who developed the communitarian economic model. Simply stated: "If the needs of the group are considered first, then the invisible hand will reach down and automatically take care of the desires of the individual."[23] List explained his economic principles in *The Natural System of Political Economy* written in 1837.

> The lessons of history justify our opposition to the assertion that states reach economic maturity most rapidly if left to their own device. . . . it may be chance that leads certain individuals to a particular place to foster the expansion of an industry that was once small and insignificant . . . . but the growth of industries is a process that may take hundreds of years to complete and one should not ascribe to sheer chance what a

> nation has achieved through its laws and
> institutions. . . . every   responsible
> government should strive to remove those
> obstacles that hinder the progress of
> civilization and should stimulate the growth
> of those economic forces that a nation
> carries in its bosom.[24]

The ideological framework drives each nation's economic policies. As the relevance of natural comparative advantages dissipates with further advances into the information age, nations are forced to embark on policies that compel the development of new comparative advantages. Nations employing the communitarian capitalism model are better fitted for developing comparative advantages that nations with the individualistic capitalism model.

This does not mean that nations, such as the United States, cannot develop new comparative advantages. They definitely can. However, this places an extraordinary burden on the government and the industry to modify the existing system or, in some cases, to completely overhaul the system. Furthermore, in the absence of government support, even more pressure is placed on the industry and individual firms to continuously create new comparative advantages.

Silicon Valley's earlier comparative advantages, as discussed previously, diminished during the 1980s. Silicon Valley still retained a proficient work force, capital, and innovative capabilities, but so did other nations and firms. If the advantages are common to all parties, then they cease to be an advantage to any given party. Furthermore, comparative advantages do not last forever. As the advantages disappear or are eroded by foreign competition, the industry and the firm have to continuously create new competitive advantages. Maintaining and creating comparative advantages requires constant and dedicated effort that should not diminish with the passage of time.

The complex process of the comparative advantage paradigm shift occurs at all levels, involves all parties, and works through different stages.

An industry can lose its comparative advantage in three ways.

1. By abandoning its current advantages.
2. By not changing current advantages or creating new advantages as economic and market situations change.

3. By letting an other industry equal or surpass their current advantages.

An industry can create advantages that allow it to successfully compete against another industry in three ways:

1. By duplicating advantages of the other industry, thus eroding the comparative advantage of that industry.
2. By exploiting comparative advantage weaknesses in the other industry, thus creating situations that diffuse the advantages of that industry.
3. By creating new advantages that are not apparent in the other industry and would be difficult for the industry to imitate or create.

The creation of comparative advantage is a four step process.

1. Developing a policy framework on comparative advantage that involves government and private sectors.
2. Identifying comparative advantages that need to be created.
3. Developing infrastructure that facilitates the process of creation and implementation.
4. Formulating detailed plans for implementation.

The shift in comparative advantage from Silicon Valley firms to Japanese firms, for example, has two patterns. The first rests squarely on the decisions, or lack of them, made by Silicon Valley firms, and the second, on the ability of Japan and its industries to create new advantages that specifically targeted the high-technology industry.

Silicon Valley firms plans and actions that permitted foreign firms to gain comparative advantages have been previously discussed in this chapter. The summary of those findings are:

• Establishing assembly plants and operations overseas that permitted the development of skilled labor and associated infrastructure in those countries that eventually competed against Silicon Valley firms.

- Providing capital and technical knowledge that enabled the development of electronics centers in various regions of the world and creating new competitors against itself.
- Licensing technology to Japanese firms who were able to acquire technologies without incurring large research and development expenses and "reverse engineering" it to create new products and technologies.
- Not developing a uniform and stable relationship with the government during inception and growth stages, thus forcing a reactive and regulatory relationship.
- Adopting traditional management practices that were developed during the 1950s and 1960s that were not relevant and compatible to the unique requirements of the microelectronics industry.
- Not actively participating in the development of local public and social infrastructure that led to dramatic increases in cost of living and business operating costs.

While all these factors contributed to the decline of Silicon Valley's comparative advantages, none was more important than the joint effort made by Japan and its industry to create comparative advantage in the industry.

The creation of comparative advantage by Japan and its industry was a carefully orchestrated plan as the process illustrates.

The first step in the process is the acceptance by Japan that it needed to create comparative advantage if it were to dominate the high-technology market. Japanese are "unwilling to accept comparative advantage as a static notion, deriving only from nature's gift. Rather, they are determined to create comparative advantage to suit national goals."[25] Paul Krugman of MIT explains that Japan has adopted "a national strategy in which government acted in concert with business to encourage certain industries."[26]

Japanese economic strategic policy was determined in the 1950s. It identified knowledge-intensive industries as the industries of the future. Although, in the 1950s Japan had the comparative advantage of cheap labor, it decided to concentrate on capital-intensive industry, forcing a "natural" shift in comparative advantage. A Japanese ministry spokesman explained:

> The Ministry of International Trade
> and Industry decided to establish in Japan
> industries which require intensive
> employment of capital and technology,
> industries that in consideration of
> comparative cost of production should be
> the most inappropriate for Japan. . . . from
> a short-run, static viewpoint,
> encouragement of such industries would
> seem to conflict with economic rationalism.
> But, from a long-range point of view, these
> are precisely the industries where income
> elasticity of demand is high.[27]

Once Japan decided to cultivate the high-technology industry, it considered the issue of financing. It evaluated four options:

1. Borrowing from foreign sources,
2. Allowing direct foreign investment by multinational corporations,
3. Pursuing state controlled and managed investment, and
4. Following a pay-as-you-go strategy.[28]

Japan rejected the first three options and pursued the fourth option of generating capital within the Japanese system. The first two options would not permit the Japanese to control their economic destiny and would make them dependent on foreign institutions. The state managed industry concept conflicted with the economic ideology of permitting private firms to compete in the marketplace. The last option made economic sense and would permit Japanese industries to control their destiny and be frugal in development efforts. The Japanese government was also relying on the typical conservational saving habits of the Japanese people that would permit the financial institutions to support new ventures.

Once the Japanese government was assured of capital, the focus was on where and how to acquire the technology. Four options were considered:

1. Japan could develop its own technology "through intensive educational programs and official sponsorship of organized science and engineering."[29]

2. Japan could import technology by "inviting high-tech American companies to build manufacturing plants in Japan, either alone or through joint-ventures."[30]
3. Japan could buy the necessary technology through licensing arrangements and royalty payments.
4. Japan could adopt a policy of "reverse engineering" by purchasing "small amounts of high-technology products, then proceed to dismantle, analyze, reengineer, and replicate these products within Japanese factories."[31]

While Japan selected all four options, it strongly emphasized the last two. These last two options provided Japanese control of the technology and, through reengineering, presented the opportunity "to leap-frog generations of intermediate technologies."[32] American firms which sold the technology to Japan "received large infusions of cash without any need for additional investment. Thus, everyone won in the short-term."[33] But, in the long-term, the principal losers were the American manufacturers "who lost significant market share to Japanese exporters."[34]

This carefully orchestrated plan conducted by the Japanese government and industry shifted the high-technology comparative advantage from Silicon Valley to Japan.

While Japan was pursuing its plan of creating new comparative advantages that would enable it do dominate the future electronics industry, it was also pursuing other options to create or maintain its advantages. The first such option concentrated on influencing United States government policy decision through lobbying and grass roots campaigns. The purpose of this strategy was "to influence the outcome of political decisions in Washington D.C. that directly affect Japanese corporate and economic interests"[35] according to Pat Choate, a Japan analyst.

The second option focused on the economic and financial weakness of Silicon Valley firms. During the height of foreign competition, Silicon Valley firms that were strapped for capital relied on Japanese investment. Through infusion of capital, Japanese firms gained access to new technologies and obtained rights to manufacture the products in Japan or in other low-cost operation areas. Since the private sector in the United States relies on private capital, many firms had no option but to accept Japanese investment and capital.

The third option restricted American firms from penetrating the Japanese market during the incubation period of the industry. As their industries become strong contenders in the global market, Japan still restricted imports. The current debate on trade barriers between Japan and United States is a culmination of this option. According to Ravi Batra, the author of *The Myth of Free Trade*, what Japan is doing is exactly what United States did during the last century to develop its new industries and protecting them from British domination.[36] Japan was following the economic ideology prescribed by Freidrich List a hundred and fifty years earlier.

The implementation of the carefully executed plan to gain comparative advantage in technology related industries is clearly evident in Japan's wresting control of the semiconductor market from Silicon Valley firms. The Semiconductor Industry Association's study in 1983 commented on the predatory industrial policy of Japan:

> In the late 1960s and early 1970s, the Japanese government protected semiconductor industry through import restraints and exclusion of foreign investment. It controlled the licensing of foreign technologies within Japan. This combination of policies was designed to keep the U.S. semiconductor industry from taking advantage of its technological leadership to establish a strong market position in Japan as it had in Europe and elsewhere. The Japanese government's efforts permitted domestic semiconductor producers to establish production capabilities and a strong domestic market position-laying the groundwork for the industry's rapid growth in the late 1970s.[37]

The study noted that Japan's Ministry of International Trade and Industry (MITI) "targeted Japan's semiconductor firms for accelerated growth,"[38] and took several steps to promulgate the growth. Some of the key steps were:

- Considerable industry-government consultation to establish industry-wide goals.
- Reorganization of the Japanese semiconductor industry in conjunction with those goals, and exempting the industry from Japan's antimonopoly laws.
- A joint industry-government R&D effort.
- Financial assistance in the form of grants and low interest loans.[39]

The comparative advantages that were created for Japanese firms are summarized in Figure 8.1.

FIGURE 8.1

COMPARATIVE ADVANTAGES ENJOYED BY TARGETED
FIRMS IN JAPAN

Information Industries and Microelectronics

Issue	Japanese Firms	Foreign Firms
Entry into Industry	Selected, subsidized, and assigned task.	Investment legally barred until 1976. Discriminatory.
Fair Trade	Exempted.	Subject to Fair Trade Laws.
Cooperative Research	Subsidize participation with technology transfer among projects.	Restricted participation and access to patents.
Financing	Japan Development Bank. Low interest loans. Normal market rates.	Restricted access to local capital.
Tax	Large first year-write-off.	Standard depreciation schedules.
Acquisition and Mergers	At MITI's discretion.	Government and Board approval.

Source: Semiconductor Industry Association

In order for Silicon Valley firms to regain comparative advantage, a concentrated plan must be embarked upon, in conjunction with government sector, to create new advantages which must then be sustained over a long period of time.

In the information and knowledge society of tomorrow, created comparative advantages will replace the natural resource comparative advantage of the past era. Silicon Valley ushered in the information era, now it must fight to maintain its dominant position.

NOTES

1. Thomas Hout, Michael E. Porter, and Eileen Rudeen, "How Global Companies Win Out," *Harvard Business Review* (September-October 1982), 98.

2. Theodore Levitt, "The Globalization of Markets," *Harvard Business Review* (May-June 1983).

3. Thomas L. Wheelan and David J. Hunger, *Strategic Management and Business Policy* (Reading: Addison-Wesley Publishing Company, 1989), 316.

4. Wheelan, *Strategic Management*, 316.

5. Levitt, *Globalization of Markets*, 92.

6. Ibid., 92.

7. Ibid., 93.

8. Ibid., 96.

9. Ibid., 96.

10. Hout, Porter, and Rudden, *How Global Companies Win Out*, 99.

11. Levitt, *Globalization of Markets*, 101.

12. Ibid., 93.

13. Gary Hamel and C.K. Prahalad, "Do You Really Have a Global Strategy?" *Harvard Business School* (July-August 1985), 139.

14. Ibid., 139.

15. Ibid., 144.

16. Hout, *How Global Companies Win Out*, 103.

17. Ibid., 103.

18. Ibid., 103.

19. Ibid., 103.

20. Peter F. Drucker, *The New Realities* (New York: Harper & Row, 1989), 129.

21. Ibid., 129.

22. Charles Hampden-Turner and Alfons Trompenaars, *The Seven Cultures of Capitalism* (New York: Doubleday, 1993), 14.

23. Ibid., 14.

24. James Fallows, "How the World Works," *The Atlantic Monthly*, December 1993, 66.

25. George C. Lodge, *Perestroika for America: Business-Government Relations for World Competitiveness* (Boston: Harvard Business School Press, 1990), 17.
26. Ibid., 17.
27. Thomas K. McCraw, ed., *America versus Japan: A Comparative Study* (Boston: Harvard Business School Press, 1986), 9.
28. Ibid., 10-12.
29. Ibid., 16.
30. Ibid., 16.
31. Ibid., 16.
32. Ibid., 17.
33. Ibid., 17.
34. Ibid., 17.
35. Pat Choate, "Political Advantage: Japan's Campaign for America," *Harvard Business Review* (September-October 1990), 87-88.
36. Ravi Batra, *The Myth of Free Trade: A Plan for America's Economic Revival* (New York: Charles Scribner's Sons, 1993).
37. *Semiconductor Industry Association*, "The Effect of Government Targeting on World Semiconductor Competition" (1993), 1.
38. Ibid., 1.
39. Ibid., 2.

Chapter 9

The Decline Analysis

> When the group or civilization declines, it is through no mystic limitation of a corporate life, but through the failure of its political or intellectual leaders to meet the challenge of change.
>
> Will and Ariel Durant
> *The Lessons of History*[1]

In a relatively short history of thirty years, Silicon Valley not only transported our society from the industrial age to the knowledge-based information society, but endured the ramifications of the change that it started. The spacious region with affordable housing, excellent living conditions, outstanding educational facilities, and easy lifestyles was transformed into a region of unaffordable housing, traffic gridlock, congested freeways, business exodus, smog and environmental problems, and an exceedingly high cost of living. Past availability of affordable skilled labor deteriorated and expensive labor costs "caused manufacturing jobs to disappear."[2] During the period from 1984 to 1991, Silicon Valley's jobs "grew less than 10 percent, less than half the national rate, the result of a net loss of some 40,000 manufacturing jobs."[3] The success of Silicon Valley came at a price.

The decline of Silicon Valley during the 1980s was not intentional or foreseen. Its success and growth created an illusion that everything was fine and that the trend would continue.

As high technology firms disappeared through failures or acquisitions, new firms emerged to take their place: "more than 85 new semiconductor firms were started in Silicon Valley during the 1980s."[4]

In the earlier chapters, it was concluded that the decline of Silicon Valley could be attributed to the loss and shift of comparative advantages that it had during its inception and growth stages. The loss of comparative advantages was caused by the shift in market economic forces, the inability of Silicon Valley firms to respond to those changes, and the deliberate actions of other nations, industries, and firms to create new comparative advantages. However, Silicon Valley's demise has been vastly exaggerated. It still retains one of the highest concentrations of "brainpower . . . and a positive mental attitude,"[5] to innovate and an ability "to think that an off-the-wall idea can turn into something big."[6] There is much to learn from the competitive regression of Silicon Valley. The lessons of failure can provide a valuable insight into the future strategies that may be needed to revitalize the industry. In the classic *Harvard Business Review* article "Strategic Intent," Hamel and Prahalad state:

> Few companies recognize the value of documenting failure. Fewer still search their own managerial orthodoxies for the seeds of competitive surrender. But we believe there is a pathology of surrender that gives some important clues.[7]

Taking a clue from the above statement, the decline of Silicon Valley can be examined from two different perspectives. The first explores the managerial orthodoxies of Silicon Valley, its own self-assessment of the decline, and review of expert commentary on the subject.

The second perspective examines and evaluates the specific actions taken by Silicon Valley to encounter its subsiding competitiveness in the global market.

DECLINE: SILICON VALLEY PERSPECTIVE

It would be readily facile to blame the decline of Silicon Valley on the economic theory of technology as expounded by Nikolai Kondratieff, a Russian economist. In his concept of the "Kondratieff cycle," he asserted that the economic impact of technology follows a fifty year cycle, at the end of which the industry is replaced by emerging technologies.[8] However, the application of this theory to the Silicon Valley problems is not that simple.

Many Silicon Valley firms discarded the original innovative characteristics that propelled them to world domination in favor of management orthodoxies and practices that focused on market share gain, short-term profit generation, and subsequently blamed external factors for its decline.

The Silicon Valley companies focused on gaining quick market shares for quick profits, rather than developing a long-term market for their products. Their goal was to beat their competitor by whatever means possible. Price cutting, hiring away people from competitors, and copying products, were just a few methods tried throughout the Valley. It was not uncommon to meet the same salesperson representing three different companies within three years.

New firms were sprouting up all over with the main aim of going public as soon as possible and making quick millionaires out of the founders and many employees. Executives were entitled to bonuses within a month of their joining the firm. This phenomenon was explained in the MIT study:

> In the American semiconductor industry a flash-in-the pan pattern has become all too familiar. First a high-tech start-up firm explodes into prominence with some brilliant initial products. . . . the early products become obsolete, and internal funds needed to finance growth decline as sales fall off and markets become more competitive. Then employees begin to defect to newer firms in order to make their own entrepreneurial fortunes.[9]

The innovative spirit in creating a new industry was replaced by the individualistic ideology of self-interest and greed. Long-range business development was replaced by short-term returns. Silicon Valley short-term orthodoxies encouraged firms to "sell or swap advanced technology to boost profits . . . and subcontract manufacturing to Japanese to reduce costs."[10]

The case history of Osborne Computers further illustrates this issue. Founded in 1981, its first year revenues were $80 million and crossed $100 million in 18 months. Yet, it declared bankruptcy in 1983, just after two years of operation. The firm created a new market niche in portable computers and gained quick market share by bundling substantial software. It was predicted that "most of the Osborne management team would be millionaires by the time they're 40 or even 30."[11]

Silicon Valley firms flooded the consumer market with new products during the late 1970s and early 1980s. Technology driven entrepreneurs were hoping to launch new "Intels" and "Apples." Many products were different versions of the similar products; many were high technology gadgets; and many had no apparent wide application. Stephen McClellan is his book *The Coming Computer Industry Shakeout* explains:

> Too many companies are selling too many products. Computer trade shows, which were once respectable, professional affairs, now resemble carnivals. . . . so many new products were announced that a new computer that seemed like a hit in the morning often found itself leapfrogged by a half-dozen competitors by midafternoon.[12]

New electronic gadgets came and went. Technical people were creating products for nontechnical consumers. Engineers controlled sales, marketing, and product distribution and were infatuated with their own product design. Greed had replaced innovation.

Most of the entrepreneurs in Silicon Valley evolved from technical backgrounds and had only limited management experience. Firms evolved around ideas and products, and management was an afterthought. The intricacies of this new industry were widely misunderstood. No one fully comprehended the impact of decreasing product life cycles, exponential product advances, and declining prices and costs. Peter Drucker explained: "The Silicon Valley high-tech entrepreneurs still operate mainly in the nineteenth-century mold."[13]

The growth of high-technology ventures demands a changing and flexible management practice. Referring to the case of Osborne Computers, the firm had a difficult time in transitioning from the entrepreneurial mode into a professionally managed corporation style. According to Robert Hartley, "the entrepreneurial personality is incompatible with the manager-type of person who must necessarily be engrossed with the nitty-gritty of details and day-to-day controls over operations."[14] Many Silicon Valley firms followed the fate of Osborne Computers.

In numerous cases the competitiveness decline problems were brought about by management itself. In a speech critical of Silicon Valley industry, T.J. Rodgers, President and CEO of Cypress Semiconductor, explained:

> I believe that approximately two-thirds of our problems are our own fault. If you are losing, you are not losing because our economic system is poor or because you are not getting government subsidies or because the Japanese are treating you unfairly. You are losing because you are being out-managed.[15]

He cited two examples of poor management in Silicon Valley: The decline of emphasis on quality was the responsibility of management and had nothing to do with external factors of decline. His next example criticized the unnecessary litigation practices of local firms. "While local companies are suing each other, our Japanese counterparts are busy shipping us exports,"[16] he stated. Intel and Advanced Micro Devices, both reputed Silicon Valley firms, have been litigating for years on design rights, costing both firms hundreds of millions of dollars.

Many industry experts have offered different reasons for the declivity of Silicon Valley. Some blame it on the short-term business attitude of managers, others on the lack of leadership, others on the failure of infrastructure, others on the economic recession, while still others blame the competitive practices of Japan. Although each of those reasons may have accounted for some of the decline, the ultimate responsibility lies in the failure of Silicon Valley to sustain and create new comparative advantages; and this involves firms, industry leaders, local public sectors, and state and federal governments.

The views of some industry analysts can be explored. Jean Deitz Sexton, author of *Silicon Valley: Inventing the Future*, asserts that Silicon Valley is "virtually without industrial leadership and direction."[17] The book suggests that America develop an industrial policy that assists Silicon Valley to regain its competitiveness.

In another fascinating analysis, Michael Malone, author of *The Big Score*, suggests that the failure of Silicon Valley is due to the breakdown of its social fabric as Silicon Valley evolved from a classless society to "an emerging class system in the once egalitarian world of Silicon Valley."[18] During its growth stage, Silicon Valley adopted a casual and informal work ethic which treated everyone alike; and "reward was based on skill, ambition and hard work, not on the roll of a collar or a knowledge of flatware."[19] The wealth creation syndrome changed, and it evolved into a class system with millionaire entrepreneurs occupying a special social structure forgetting that "for every multimillionaire there are probably a thousand people who helped create that wealth."[20] The author concluded that Silicon Valley "is hardening into a rigid class system; and with that ossification will come the inevitable result-envy, hatred, even class warfare."[21] The strength of synergy and a common purpose to innovate does not exist anymore. It had lost its advantage.

A study conducted by SRI International, a reputed research firm in Silicon Valley, faulted the infrastructure breakdown for the Silicon Valley's economic deterioration.[22] The study asserted that the failure of job and business creation was "due largely to such factors as the high cost of housing, burdensome business regulations and congested transportation arteries."[23] Another expert concurred with SRI's contention. Lenny Siegel, director of the Pacific Studies Center, agreed: "Silicon Valley's problems are those of unplanned, rapid growth, not economic stagnation."[24]

The critics of the above SRI study rather assign the failure on the overall economic decline in the American electronics industry and "to the initial bust in the personal computer industry in the mid-1980s . . . the maturity of that industry, the semiconductor industry and other electronic sectors."[25] It is easy to ascribe the decline and failure of Silicon Valley to external economic factors and the industry life cycle, because this absolves the valley of the blame. Anyone who thinks that this industry has matured has a very limited technology horizon. The electronics economic recession, if there is such a thing since the businesses still continued to grow during the 1980s, does not explain why some local and foreign firms continued their growth and success.

Yet another analysis attributes the decline on the dereliction of Silicon Valley's core values brought about by the venture capitalist industry. The financial investors push the "companies to grow fast and attain liquidity early in their lives,"[26] usually through initial public offering. Silicon Valley firms, in effect, act as investment portfolios, not as creators of new technologies and markets. Technical entrepreneurs create products not markets. Silicon Valley's values migrated from an innovative model to a "purely economic model," that "lacks an underpinning of core values and deeper purpose;"[27] subsequently reducing the business to not more than a money-making machine. Silicon Valley entrepreneurs, required to acquire capital from venture capitalists, were obligated to deliver a quick economic return, not build a lasting industry. The Silicon Valley paradigm shifted from creating long-term businesses to generating short-term returns on investment. Although businesses are brought into being to make money, "to build an enduring, great company requires more than economic motives."[28]

If these evaluations are not sufficiently causative, there exists the ultimate blame for failure: Japan. Many industry leaders, business analysts, and even local media commentators condemn Japan and Japanese firms for Silicon Valley's downslide. It represents an easy target. Silicon Valley has criticized Japan's predatory tactics, Japanese government/industry collusion, product dumping, and stealing American technologies. What Silicon Valley has failed to understand and refuses to understand is that Japan and its industry operates under a different set of ideologies and business practices. The decline of Silicon Valley is not caused by the economic and industrial policies of Japan, but rather the failure of the Silicon Valley industry to understand the Japanese economic system and style of conducting business. Americans generally believe that all free-market capitalistic systems follow the American model.

A fascinating series of three articles written by James Fallows in *The Atlantic Monthly*,[29] analyzes the failure of Silicon Valley firms against their Japanese competitors. He dismisses the familiar excuse of different ethnic and culture values of both countries. He accepts that some of the blame can be ascribed to the manner in which businesses are managed, quality issues, and short-term thinking on the part of managers. Nevertheless, he contends that, unlike Japan, the major reason is the lack of American government involvement in the industry. He argues that active government involvement "is often considered an embarrassing afterthought in American discussions on how economies should work."[30] However forceful his argument, it still does not spell out the real reason and that is the loss of comparative advantage by Silicon Valley firms. He compares the different ideologies and recommends that our businesses must understand that we are not competing in similar free-market capitalist environments. It is true that the Japanese government plays an active role in industrial development, but it still allows the industry to compete. A government does not guarantee or ensure superior quality products, high-productivity, participative management, and continuous process innovation. That is the responsibility of the business. Government can create a positive environment in which the industry grows and flourishes, but, it cannot ensure substitutes for efficient business practices. As Paul Krugman, the noted MIT economist, maintains: in the end it is a business entity that has to compete in the world marketplace, not the government.[31] Neither does James Fallows offer any suggestions as to how the industry should rebuild its comparative advantage.

Silicon Valley's decline cannot be explained by all the above reasons. All the above factors have precipitated the erosion of comparative advantages. Silicon Valley has no choice but to create new advantages for the future.

DECLINE: SILICON VALLEY RESPONSE

Silicon Valley industrialists knew that they were facing competitive pressures in domestic and international markets. They had to act in order to prevent the continued erosion of their market share. They responded through the creation of their own support and lobbying groups, business alliances, and private/public joint ventures.

The intent of these measures was to defend the industry against overseas competition and to regain the market leadership position. They were reactive responses, not conceived for the development of a national technology or industrial policy, but for the purpose of ensuring the survival of the industry and individual firms in the industry.

The first response was the development of membership associations, comprised of high-technology firms, that would promote and lobby for their particular industry. The second approach was the forming of strategic business alliances to create technology advantage. The third tactic involved joint government/industry ventures to generate new competitive advantages.

Support Associations

Two support membership associations were chartered to promote specific industry segments. The associations represented membership issues and interests through lobbying activities. The associations were: the American Electronics Association (AEA) and the Semiconductor Industry Association (SIA).

American Electronics Association (AEA)

The American Electronic Association was formed in Silicon Valley in the early 1970s. Its "legislative goal is to provide a healthy business environment for the electronics industry in California and to strengthen the industry's position in world markets."[32] Its total membership comprises more than 3,500 companies which contribute an annual fee for the privilege of being part of this association. The fee is based on company's annual revenues: thus larger companies pay higher membership fees and consequently command higher clout within the association.

The industry members employ over 600,000 workers in California, with an annual payroll of $19 billion and produce goods and services of more than $64 billion, making it the largest manufacturing sector in the state.

The association is issue-oriented. It supports a broad range of issues at the state and federal level in order to promote the interests of the industry. With its headquarters in Silicon Valley, it maintains offices in both capitals: Washington D.C. and Sacramento, California.

Some of the key issues that it promotes at the federal government level are investment tax credits for research and development, science and technology policy, trade and tariff issues, and intellectual property protection.[33]

At the California state level, it argues for fiscal policy issues, environmental policy issues, education policy, and human resources issues.[34]

It is important to have an association representing the issues of the industry. It is common throughout the world. The problem with such an association is that it represents a reactive response to competitive challenge. Despite the fact that the association came into existence during the 1970s, it is still unable to do anything to assist Silicon Valley during the 1980s decline.

AEA's ideology, which is based on the American and Silicon Valley ideology, ignores and misunderstands the global competitive environment. It supports the individualistic ideology: "economic growth and productivity improvements result from the vision and genius of the individuals and companies who have the courage to take risks and attract the financial resources necessary to explore new ideas."[35] This ideology also ignores today's global environment when there are economic nations and economic blocks that are as strong and stable as those of the United States. AEA also does not believe in government-led industrial targeting or industrial policy but does believe that government support can assist the industry. That is a dichotomy.

Since AEA's financial revenues, which are membership fees, are based on the size of the firm, it tends to focus on the interests of the larger firms in the industry. New and small firms do not join the association partly because they cannot afford it and partly because they do not receive equal attention in the association. The association, driven by the need to maintain a positive cash flow, has not developed a policy framework for the assistance of new entrepreneurial firms, the type of firms that launched Silicon Valley to prominence in the first place.

As long as AEA remains an issue-oriented support group, its long-term positive impact on Silicon Valley is questionable.

Semiconductor Industry Association (SIA)

In order for an industry to gain political advantage in Washington D.C., executives in the industry must band together for action. If government's involvement is necessary to maintain industry competitiveness, then the industry must collectively resort to political activism to get desired results. The Semiconductor Industry Association was formed in 1977 to do just that.

Most of the semiconductor companies were formed by capitalists-entrepreneurs dedicated to self-reliance, free trade, and no government intervention.

During the vigorous competitive environment in the 1980s, the semiconductor industry accused Japanese firms of illegal trade practices. Japanese erosion of their world market share forced the semiconductor firms to band together and seek government intervention on their behalf. SIA started its campaign in June 1985, when it filed a formal request "for relief under Section 301 of the Trade Act of 1974 which authorizes the President of the United States to penalize countries that deny U.S. products fair access to their markets."[36]

Through intensive lobbying, the U.S. government administration was convinced; and in April 1987, it approved $300 million in punitive sanctions against Japan. The new accord forced the Japanese to open its markets to United States semiconductor companies. This was a rare example of the American government and industry working together. The successful SIA lobbying effort is attributed to the fact that the companies in the association presented a united front and were fully supported by the industry's leaders.[37]

However, this isolated success needs to be evaluated in the proper focus. The united front by the industry was forced after the semiconductor companies' market share declined against the Japanese firms. The same American firms had earlier licensed their technologies to the Japanese firms in the hope of penetrating foreign markets in exchange for royalty revenues. This is typical of the business myopia of short-term thinking. If the industry leaders had envisioned long-range ramifications of their decisions, they would have realized that licensing technology to the Japanese would eventually hurt the industry and the American economy, which is what happened. There is also a further question as to whether the punitive measures that were leveled against Japan would not lead to retaliation.[38] In an interdependent economy, American industry is also dependent on Japanese for much of its semiconductor components. In a provocative book, *Japan That Can Say No*, Shintaro Ishihara suggested that Japan should deny selling certain components if it hurts the Japanese economy.[39] In the opinion of some authorities punitive measures lead to further trade problems.

The forming of the association to represent the industry's interests has advantages. SIA has done an excellent job of analyzing the semiconductor markets, trends, and shifts in technology; and that information has been readily made available to industry members. However, it still remains an issue-oriented lobbying association reacting to economic and competitive shifts.

It is obvious that both associations have worked aggressively to assist the industry after it got into trouble, but both have been unsuccessful in working with federal and state governments in developing a long-range industrial policy that would benefit the industry before it gets into trouble. Once the competitor gains market dominance, it becomes a daunting task to unseat the leader. Silicon Valley industries should ensure that they do not lose their leadership position again. Such foresight can only happen if the plans and policies are construed prior to the industry slipping from its leadership position.

Strategic Alliance

To respond to foreign competition, some American companies decided to form a technological strategic alliance to regain competitive edge. While the federal government supported the concept, no one was certain as to whether this concept would really work. Sharing and developing technology was new to the microelectronics industry, especially when the participants in the alliance were fierce competitors. They were forced to work together not because of mutual admiration, but to strengthen their technological competitive edge against the Japanese firms. To prevent further decline of their competitiveness, they were willing to overlook their past differences.

U.S. Memories is one such alliance: On June 22, 1989, *The New York Times* announced the formation of a memory chip consortium of seven firms. The news bulletin read, "Citing the critical need for domestic production of computer memory chips, seven

American semiconductor and computer manufacturers have banded together to finance the establishment of U.S. Memories Inc."[40] The foundation charter of this coalition was based on the production of dynamic random access memory chips, or DRAMs, the most commonly used chip in electronics. The group included IBM, which would provide the technology, and six other manufacturers in the electronics industry: Hewlett-Packard, Intel, Advanced Micro Devices, Digital Equipment, LSI Logic, and National Semiconductor. The seven firms made an initial investment of $50,000 each and pledged another $500 million of the total $1 billion proposed for the project. Sanford Kane of IBM, who was hired as U.S. Memories' chief executive officer, said: "The time is right for a collective memory manufacturing in what is truly a critical technology."[41] Motorola and Texas Instruments did not participate in the alliance because they were already producing the DRAMs. The high capital investment required for manufacturing would be shared by the alliance members; and they would collectively buy the product from this joint venture.

The alliance made sense in that it would supply the product for exactly those domestic and international markets which were dominated by the Japanese. The new venture would also be able to pool research and development knowledge and progress in technology. On June 22, 1989, the *San Jose Mercury* endorsed the alliance as it would "guarantee a domestic supply of computer chips, and the proposal would bring together fierce competitors"[42] to present a joint front in competing against the Japanese domination in the DRAM market. Invented by Intel, Silicon Valley semiconductor firms monopolized the DRAM world market just 15 years ago. After the Japanese obtained the licensing rights to technology and manufacturing, they bypassed the American counterparts and gained complete domination of the market. In view of the market situation and the importance of DRAMs for computer products, the alliance made sense.

Unfortunately, on January 24, 1990, *The New York Times* reported:

> The joint venture formed last year to
> rescue the American computer industry
> from the clutches of the Japanese chip cartel
> died of financial anemia last week. The

giant companies it was intended to protect
just could not bring themselves to sign
checks amounting to a few days' worth of
the industry's annual investment budget.[43]

The big seven cartel neglected to come up with the money
previously agreed upon although the amount of funding was only a
very small element of their budgets. Gary Saxonhouse, a specialist on
the Japanese economy at the University of Michigan, commented that:
"High-tech manufacturers are happy to play the us-versus-them game
on the public's nickel. But with their own money at stake they are far
more likely to look to the bottom line."[44]

If it indeed were a great idea jointly supported by the industry
and the government, why did it not succeed? American business
ideology of free-market competition could not unite the companies to
benefit the industry in the long-term. The American government
played only a passive role in the venture. Sanford Kane, President of
U.S. Memories, criticized the consortium members: "These guys have
a tactical view of the world; they don't think strategically." They
were able "to so quickly forget that a year ago they were screaming
for this."[45] Sharing technology and presenting a joint front is not the
strength of semiconductor firms. Because each firm opted to compete
alone in the market and felt that their investment in their own research
and development would be more beneficial that pooling of individual
talent. Consequently the industry lost the DRAM market to the
Japanese.

As of today there still is no successful industry alliance. If
Silicon Valley is to create future advantages, it must rethink its ability
to join forces if required.

Government/Industry Joint Alliance

Virtually all industrial nations, except the United States, have
developed and implemented an industrial policy to enhance the
competitiveness of their electronic industries. Government and
industry in those countries have jointly sponsored research and
development projects.

SEMATECH,   the   SEmiconductor   MAnufacturing
TECHnology initiative,   is   an   industry/government-sponsored
consortium   designed   to   promote   America's   preeminence   in

semiconductor manufacturing technology.[46] It was formed in 1987 "as a novel partnership between 14 electronics companies and the U.S. government with the goal of improving the semiconductor industry's ability to manufacture and compete."[47] The consortium was formed in response to the declining U.S. competitiveness in world markets. Many analysts viewed this as "too little and too late." It was agreed by the members of the group that the United States must regain leadership in semiconductor technology—the foundation of its largest industry, electronics—if it were to remain a competitive international power.

While the industry was responding to declining profits, the government was becoming concerned for national security reasons. A Department of Defense task force commented in February 1987, that the American armed forces depend heavily on technological superiority from semiconductor-based electronics in order to prevail. The task force was apprehensive about the dependency on foreign suppliers for the high-tech components; and it urged the government to pursue the venture with great urgency.[48]

Although Sematech was conceived as a consortium to assist the American economy, industry, and technology, each member firm, and also the government, were more concerned about their individual needs.

The operating budget was about $250 million per year, half contributed by the member companies and half from federal, state, and local governments. In effect, this was truly a joint government/business project.

During the next three years, Sematech spent much of its time and its annual budget on research grants and programs to help the battered semiconductor equipment industry make better products. William Spencer, chief executive of Sematech, announced, "Now is the time for industry and government to capitalize on our momentum. We have an opportunity to concentrate on building a sustainable, competitive infrastructure. Sematech has shown that generic, pre-competitive cooperation can work in America."[49] It also announced a 5-year plan in 1991. The plan was welcomed by the industry. The alliance looked too good to be true.

In December 1991, the following news item appeared in the *San Jose Mercury News*: "Milpitas firm quits Sematech venture. Others may follow LSI Logic's lead."[50]

The breakdown of the alliance had started. The explanation from LSI Logic was that due to business slowdown it had to decide whether to continue to invest in Sematech or lay off workers. The criticism of the alliance was that it strayed away from its initial objective and was spending most of its money bailing out a "beleaguered semiconductor equipment industry."[51] The Sematech saga is another example of a failed government/business alliance. Though the intentions were worthy, the response was dispensed too late, and was principally directed toward assisting troubled firms. Because the consortium members were more concerned about their own individual profits and survival than that of the industry as a whole, short-term business thinking and constant focus on the bottom-line rendered the government-industry alliance virtually unworkable in the United States. Though SEMATECH still exists, its effectiveness has been diminished; and it has not achieved any major results for the industry.

Silicon Valley formed yet another alliance called Joint Venture: Silicon Valley. Its mission statement is:

> A landmark collaboration of leading economic interests in the Silicon Valley committed to developing a workable plan for regional economic growth and renewal. The objective of this unprecedented community-wide effort will be to construct a rational blueprint for the continued economic vitality of the Silicon Valley as it enters a new era of fierce global competition.
>
> Joint Venture: Silicon Valley will achieve its objectives by seeking out the broadest possible range of insights and perspectives from organizations and individuals throughout the regions.[52]

This alliance has provided positive support to Silicon Valley. It has initiated incubators and support for new ventures, which are the lifeblood of Silicon Valley. It has addressed some key issues, such as, high cost of doing business in California, education, and improving the quality of life. Operating with limited resources and authority, whether this venture will achieve long-term success still remains to be seen.

It is apparent that most of the strategic alliances that have been formed have not been successful. Considerable time and expense have been consumed. Why do these well-intentioned alliances fade away? A few key reasons are noted:

- Nearly all the alliances have been formed as an after-thought only after the industry started to face competitive decline. There was no consensus planning during the industry's growth stage to plan the future of the industry if and when it faced competition. The alliances were reactive responses to problems.
- The alliances were issue-oriented and were created to protect the industry through legislative actions, rather than creating a policy framework that would place the industry in a long-term strong competitive position.
- The alliances mostly focused on the problems of the specific segments of the industry and the problems of individual firms.
- There was no consensus among the alliance members and partners on the ventures. The alliances were pulled in all directions to satisfy the individual requirements of its members.
- The alliances focused on large firms and generally ignored the needs of ascending entrepreneurial firms, the type of firms that launched the Silicon Valley in the first place.
- The American economic ideology prevented the alliances and support organization from agreeing on the need for an industrial or technology policy, much less on what type of policy to have.
- Most of the alliance members were inexperienced in working together and were driven by their own individual needs and not the needs of the industry in the global competitive environment.

There is an important lesson in the responses taken by Silicon Valley firms. If the Valley is to retain its position as the leading microelectronic center in the world and create new and continuous comparative advantages, then it must relearn its business thinking and must foster cooperation and coordination to remain a viable force in the world markets.

NOTES

1. Will and Ariel Durant, *The Lessons of History* (New York: Simon and Schuster, 1968), 92.

2. Richard Brandt, *Business Week*, Enterprise 1993, 175.

3. Ibid., 175.

4. AnnaLee Saxenian, "Regional Networks and the Resurgence of Silicon Valley," *California Management Review* (Fall 1990), 89.

5. Brandt, *Business Week*, Enterprise 1993, 170.

6. Ibid., 170.

7. Gary Hamel and C.K. Prahalad, "Strategic Intent," *Harvard Business Review* (May-June 1989), 71.

8. Peter Drucker, *Innovation and Entrepreneurship*, (New York: Harper Business, 1993), 4-5.

9. Michael L. Dertouzous, Richard K. Lester, and Robert M. Solow, *Made in America: Regaining the Productive Edge* (New York: Harper Perennial, 1989), 9.

10. Ibid., 251.

11. Robert F. Hartley, *Management Mistakes* (New York: John Wiley & Sons, 1986), 218.

12. Stephen T. McClellan, *The Coming Computer Industry Shakeout: Winners, Losers, and Survivors* (New York: John Wiley & Sons, 1984), 27-28.

13. Drucker, *Innovation and Entrepreneurship*, 12.

14. Hartley, *Management Mistakes*, 222.

15. Speech by T.J. Rodgers to American Electronics Association, Seattle Washington, 12 May 1990.

16. Ibid.

17. *San Jose Mercury News*, 1991.

18. Michael S. Malone, "A capital offense: Class comes to the valley," *San Jose Mercury News*, 13 May 1990, 1C and 5C.

19. Ibid., 1C.

20. Ibid., 5C.

21. Ibid., 5C.

22. Steve Kaufman, "Study questions origin of Silicon Valley slump," *San Jose Mercury News*, 28 June 1992, 1E.

23. Ibid., 1E.

24. Lenny Siegel, "Valley Future," *San Jose Mercury News*, 3 January 1993, 1C.
25. Kaufman, *San Jose Mercury News*, 28 June 1992.
26. James C. Collins, "Silicon Valley's big myth," *San Jose Mercury News*, 28 June 1992, 1C and 8C.
27. Ibid., 8C.
28. Ibid., 8C.
29. James Fallows, "Looking at the Sun," November 1993; "How the World Works," December 1993; and "What is an Economy For?" November 1993, *The Atlantic Monthly*.
30. Fallows, "Looking at the Sun," *The Atlantic Monthly*, November 1993, 90.
31. Paul Krugman, "Competitiveness: A Dangerous Obsession," *Foreign Affairs* (March/April 1994).
32. *American Electronic Association*
33. *American Electronic Association*, "America's Future at Stake: Winning in the Global Marketplace."
34. *American Electronics Association*, "Sacramento Caucus," (7 February 1990).
35. *American Electronic Association*, "America's Future at Stake," 16.
36. David B. Yoffie, "How An Industry Builds Political Advantage: Silicon Valley goes to Capitol Hill," *Harvard Business Review* (May-June 1988), 83.
37. Ibid., 83.
38. *Harvard Business School*, "The Semiconductor Industry Association and the Trade Dispute with Japan," (11 March 1991), 10.
39. Akio Morita and Shintaro Ishihara, *The Japan That Can Say No*.
40. Lawrence M. Fischer, "7 Makers Plan Chip Venture," *New York Times*, 22 June 1989.
41. Ibid.
42. Mike Langberg, "Antitrust objections called unlikely," *San Jose Mercury News*, 22 June 1989.
43. Peter Passell, "U.S. Memories: Who is the Loser?" *New York Times*, 24 January 1990.
44. Ibid.
45. Fallows, *The Atlantic Monthly*, November 1993, 81.

46. *SEMATECH*, "Executive Summary: Meeting America's Technology Challenge," ES-1.
47. Valerie Rice, "Sematech unveils 5-year plan," *San Jose Mercury News*, 1991.
48. "Sematech," *Harvard Business School*, 13-15.
49. *San Jose Mercury News*, 1991.
50. Valerie Rice, "Milpitas firm quits Sematech venture," *San Jose Mercury News*, December 1991, 1A.
51. Ibid., 8A.
52. "Joint Venture: Silicon Valley," *The Business Journal*, San Jose, August 1992.

Chapter 10

The Renewal Of Silicon Valley:
Creating New Advantages

> I believe we are at the beginning of a new era for Silicon Valley. . . . in the mid-1990s, we have many strengths to get it going. We have the best and the brightest computer scientists in the world. Our innovative and entrepreneurial spirit is alive and thriving. We have world-class manufacturing and research and development organizations. And our educational establishments continue to rank among the very best. . . . there is a new awareness that reinvention of the corporation in Silicon Valley is going to go on forever. . . . our mission is to continue to reinvent Silicon Valley so it continues to be a vital global force as we approach the end of the century.[1]
>
> Ed McCracken
> *CEO, Silicon Graphics*

Silicon Valley firms started their recovery and resurgence in 1993. Local firms grew faster than most of the country's largest corporations. According to the *San Jose Mercury News*, "sales for the 100 largest companies rose 17.5 percent to $91.2 billion from $77.6

billion last year. Profits for the top 100 firms rose 36 percent to a record $4.58 billion from $3.37 billion last year."[2] The success of 1993 was repeated in 1994 and 1995. Simultaneously, another news item in the same newspaper noted that Silicon Valley firms "previously faced little or no competition are restructuring to cut labor costs as the field of competitors becomes more crowded."[3] While some Silicon Valley firms are experiencing growth in revenues, others are terminating employees. At the same time as the semiconductor firms are doing well, computer and software firms are struggling. This situation changed in 1995 and 1996 when the semiconductor companies, except Intel, were struggling, but software companies involved in Internet, communications, multimedia, and networking were doing well. New companies, like Yahoo and Netscape, were creating new records in initial public offering.

However, this growth should be reviewed in the right context. First, the microelectronics industry is still the largest growing industry in the world and there still exist many opportunities for growth. Second, most of the developed nations are just now recovering from an economic recession while the American economy has been robust for the past two years. Most developed nations lag the American economic cycle. Third, the semiconductor firms' growth is partly caused by increased demand from telecommunication and multimedia industries. Fourth, the Valley firms are realizing productivity gain through the application of technology and information systems. Finally, new firms are materializing because of the convergence of computers, communications, and entertainment. Because these new companies create new markets, "Silicon Valley will face ever-increasing competition as other parts of the world, and the country, try to imitate our success."[4] Silicon Valley is still in a strong position to "benefit as technology continues to change rapidly and high-technology companies become an ever-increasingly important part of the world economy."[5]

This chapter discusses the reasons for the Silicon Valley to reposition itself for the future, reviews expert advice for its renewal, and, finally, provides a managerial framework for it to create and sustain new comparative advantages.

WHY MUST SILICON VALLEY REINVENT ITSELF?

There are two major reasons why Silicon Valley needs to resurrect itself for the future. Firstly, it is functioning in a vastly different global economic competitive environment than it did twenty years ago. It is no longer the dominant or sole proprietor of innovation. It faces increased competition from other international firms in domestic, foreign, and emerging markets of developing countries, which have equal access to technology, capital, and resources.

Secondly, technology has forced a major transformation in the functioning and operations of business organizations. The business management practices of the past are no longer relevant. Downsizing and shrinking managerial hierarchies are examples of work transformation. *Fortune*, in its feature article on the computer revolution, concluded: "More than any other agent of change, information technology is transforming the way business works."[6] Silicon Valley, like the rest of the business world, needs to adapt to these changes.

Peter Drucker describes the organization of the future:

> The typical business will be knowledge-based, an organization composed largely of specialists who direct and discipline their own performance through organized feedback from colleagues, customers, and headquarters. For this reason, it will be what I call an information-based organization.[7]

The shift from the old concept of labor, capital, and natural resources as the means of production to the resource of the future, knowledge, has created the new type of worker, called "knowledge worker." In Drucker's words: "The economic challenge of the post-capitalist society will therefore be the productivity of knowledge work and the knowledge worker."[8]

Kenichi Ohmae, who is regarded as the Peter Drucker of Japan, predicts that future businesses will have to rely on alliances. In his book, *The Borderless World*, he states: "Today's products rely on so many different critical technologies that most companies can no longer maintain a lead in all of them," thus forcing alliances around the world, and "no company can keep all critical technologies out of the hands of competitors around the globe."[9]

Technology has created a revolution in business productivity, forcing redesigning of business systems and organization structures. As *Business Week* analyzed: "But the real breakthrough isn't just in technology. It's the sweeping changes in management and organizational structure that are redefining how work gets done."[10]

As Silicon Valley forges ahead towards the twenty-first century, it must redesign itself in conformance with the new economic and technology realities. Furthermore, the many new and upcoming business entrants in Silicon Valley need to understand the new paradigm shift and organize and structure themselves accordingly.

WHAT THE EXPERTS ADVISE

Many experts have offered suggestions on reinventing American and Silicon Valley businesses. In *Short-Term America*, Michael Jacobs argues for curing the "myopic underpinning" of American businesses and demands changes in American business ideology as a cure for permanent shift away from the short-term profit focus.[11]

Charles Handy, author of The *Age of Unreason*, suggests that "we break out of traditional ways of thinking in order to use change to our advantage,"[12] and offers different organization scenarios.

Lester Thurow argues for developing and investing in "a high-quality, well-motivated work force interested in working together as a team to raise productivity."[13]

Homa Bahrani prescribes "developing a flexible organization . . . a multi-dimensional concept-demanding agility and versatility; associated with change, innovation, and novelty; coupled with robustness and resilience, implying stability, sustainable advantage, and capabilities that may evolve over time."[14]

Peter Drucker advises managers "to learn to manage in situations where you don't have command authority, where you are neither controlled nor controlling;"[15] be prepared to assume more individual responsibility rather than depend on the company; and, "must be both managers of specialists and synthesizers of different fields of knowledge."[16]

Edward McCracken, chief executive officer of Silicon Graphics, a successful Silicon Valley firm, proclaims that future organizations will not only operate in chaos, but also produce chaos. He advises:

> The key to obtaining competitive advantage in the 1990s is making your customers feel like you designed a product specifically for them, that your product has special features or capabilities for which they would pay a premium. It's difficult to add value if you're removed from your customers.[17]

He suggests continuous innovation in high-technology firms and recommends a very close relationship between technologists and customers.

Prescriptions offered include: developing cross-functional teams; maintaining strong relationships with customers; utilizing the virtual corporation concept that extends the corporation's working boundaries by creating value-added products; and reengineering the corporation, which means "starting all over, starting from scratch."[18]

There is a definite demand to change. However, what Silicon Valley needs is a unique Silicon Valley solution. It definitely had comparative advantages in the past, and it definitely can create new comparative advantages in the future. As Michael Porter suggests:

> Companies achieve competitive advantage through acts of innovation. They approach innovation in its broadest sense, including both new technologies and new ways of doing things. They perceive a new basis for competing or find better means of competing in old ways. Innovation can be manifested in a new product design, a new production process, or a new way of conducting training.[19]

Silicon Valley has never been accused of lacking in innovation. But innovation in technology and products should be supplanted by innovation in management practices and creative business strategies. Each firm needs to ascertain its own competitive advantage for its markets and decide which managerial system to adopt. Industry's competitiveness "results from convergence of the management practices and organizational modes favored in the country and the sources of competitive advantage in the industry."[20]

For Silicon Valley to create new comparative advantages and then be in a position to continuously evaluate, modify, and create new advantages, a new managerial frame of mind is required. Only when management realizes that it has to make the changes, why it has to make those changes, and what it must do to make those changes, can lasting results be achieved. No change can happen without active management participation at all levels of the organization. The successful Silicon Valley firm in the future will thrive on the dynamism of change and be organizationally positioned to continuously create and respond to change.

The four elements that are essential in reinventing and maintaining new comparative advantages are:

1. Shifting managerial frames of reference to accept the new realities of global economic competitive environment.
2. Learning to operate in a new marketing paradigm.
3. Creating a new model of strategic business thinking.
4. Developing a consistent long-term partnership with local and federal government.

CHANGING MANAGERIAL FRAMES OF REFERENCE

The first and foremost challenge facing Silicon Valley managers is adjusting to the new economic and competitive realities. Changing managerial frames of reference entails discarding old management concepts about competition, markets, and economics. Managerial frame of reference is defined as "the assumptions, premises, and accepted wisdom that bound or 'frame' a company's understanding of itself and its industry."[21] Managers acquire these frames of reference from academia, business practices, peers, advisors, and ideological upbringing. These frames of reference invisibly drive the "company's approach to competitive warfare and thus determine competitive outcomes."[22] According to a *Harvard Business School* article: "long-term competitiveness depends on the managers' willingness to challenge continually their managerial frames."[23] The authors, Gary Hamel and C.K. Prahalad assert that:

> Global competition is not just product versus product, company versus company, or trading bloc versus trading bloc. It is mind-set versus mind-set, managerial frame versus managerial frame.[24]

What the authors are alluding to is that the future competitive environment not only requires understanding of products, firms, and industries, but also of economic and business ideologies.

The first component of management relearning is that Silicon Valley firms do not have a monopoly on technology; they are not the only providers of goods and services, and that they compete against firms that may be more powerful and richer in resources than themselves. As Arthur Money, president of ESL, commented on Silicon Valley's competitive realities: "We're now one of many, and we're having to learn about new players . . . we're in the information age, where knowledge and ability, not merely force of capital, are determining factors,"[25] in global competitiveness.

In the book *Ideology and National Competitiveness*, George Lodge explains the economic shift:

> Competition in world trade is among nations as well as firms, and national governments compete to make their jurisdictions the most hospitable locations for global production systems. And comparative advantage is by no means God given; it is created by the nation through collective action following the dictates of a national strategy laid down by government in close collaboration with business and labor.[26]

A typical American manager's frame of reference embodies a free market economy where firms compete with each other without the interference of the government. Unfortunately, that is not the case with other nations. In most countries, governments play a participative and/or active role in changing firms' competitive positions. To change and relearn, Silicon Valley managers must understand different economic and business ideologies. Customarily American business education teaches with analytical tools developed during the age of domestic competition. International competition is much different. Exposing managers to other ideologies makes them examine "their own ideological assumptions along with the ideology of other nations thus discloses to managers a broader range of possible responses."[27]

Limiting the managerial frame of mind to only one ideological framework poses a serious dilemma for managers creating adversarial repercussions instead of constructive relationships. Silicon Valley's relationship with government is an example. Ezra Vogel explains:

> Many leaders in government and business deal with issues only within the limited framework of their personal ideological assumptions without subjecting them to critical examinations. American managers ideologically blinded to a range of responses consistent with communitarian ideology may find themselves locked into adversarial relationships with government and labor on issues that require more flexible and cooperative relationships.[28]

This ideological perspective prevented Silicon Valley and government from working together to develop a cohesive plan to counter the Japanese competitive threat in semiconductors. Had the government and the industry cooperated at the onset of industry's development, the situation might have been prevented.

The American business ideology dominates its business thinking. Much has been written about the short-term perspective of American businesses. According to Michael Jacobs, "the primary cause of business myopia is the distant relationship between the providers of capital (shareholders and lenders) and the users of capital (corporate managers)."[29] Since the investors are detached from the businesses, they evaluate the business on short-term financial results.

One of the contributing reasons for Silicon Valley's decline was the emphasis on introducing new products to grow rapidly so that the investors could receive large monetary gains at the time of initial public offerings.

Unless Silicon Valley management shifts its frames of reference from short-term economic gains to a long-range perspective on business investment, its ability to compete in the global economy will be severely curtailed. The only way to accomplish the shift in the managerial frames of reference is through appropriate business education that confronts the new ideological and business realities of the global competition. In a scathing review of business education, *The Wall Street Journal* commented:

> There is a need for a fundamental rethinking of graduate management education. Given the increasing demographic diversity of the workplace, fast changing technologies and the internationalization of business, simply preparing students to solve problems in traditional ways is insufficient.[30]

Silicon Valley managers require new thinking and unlearning of the deeply entrenched business practices and ideologies. Past industry success makes it difficult to discard the old managerial frames of reference.

CREATING A NEW MARKETING PARADIGM

Silicon Valley's growth occurred during the period when the demand for its products far exceeded what it could supply. The market size was huge, and Silicon Valley firms faced limited competition. It is easy to deal when the demand is high and no competition exists. Silicon Valley firms never truly learned the art of marketing their products in a competitive environment. The situation today is different. There are many new competitors, new markets are emerging, and emerging technologies are continuously redefining industries.

The new marketing paradigm requires that firms chart a marketing course that enables them to overcome ideological, cultural, social, political, environmental, economic, and business barriers. Technology changes are creating new products and services that require new customers in untested markets. Creating the best product, offering it at competitive prices, having the best price/performance ratio, and outstanding quality, though essential, are not sufficient reasons for entering and creating new markets. Silicon Valley firms are now challenged to create a new marketing paradigm for the future.

Global corporations, in an attempt to trade their products on a worldwide basis, are faced with overcoming markets that are blocked. This blockage is caused by several factors, ranging from the inability to access a distribution system to cultural preferences or government laws.

To overcome this blockage, Phil Kotler developed the concept of megamarketing. He defined megamarketing as the ability to "gain market access in order to satisfy human demand and/or to create or alter consumer demand."[31] Figure 10.1 illustrates the difference between traditional marketing and megamarketing in terms of their objectives, the parties and personnel involved, marketing tools used, inducements, time frame, and investment.

FIGURE 10.1

MARKETING AND MEGAMARKETING CONTRASTED[32]

	Marketing	Megamarketing
Marketing Objective	To satisfy consumer demand.	To gain market access in order to satisfy consumer demand or to create or alter consumer demand.
Parties Involved	Consumers, distributors, dealers, suppliers, marketing firms.	Normal parties plus legislatures, government agencies, labor unions, reform groups, general public.
Marketing tools	Market research, product development, pricing, distribution planning, promotion.	Normal tools plus the use of power and public relations.
Type of Inducement	Positive and official inducements	Positive inducements (official and unofficial) and negative inducements.
Time frame	Short	Much longer
Investment cost	Low	Much higher
Personnel	Marketers	Marketers plus company officers, lawyers, public relations, public affairs.

Megamarketing recognizes the need to employ power and public relations and the ability to influence government agencies and other branches of government in order to unlock market barriers. The concept recognizes the need for significant investment, long-term time frame, and the involvement of company paid lobbyists and executive officers in addition to personnel within the marketing and sales areas.

Pat Choate, in his article "Political Advantage: Japan's Campaign for America" describes the use by Japan of Kotler's megamarketing concept. Choate reports that by investing approximately $800 million each year, Japan is able to support one thousand Washington D.C. lobbyists, develop a grass roots political network, and influence politicians by contributing to their campaigns.[33] This investment, Choate states, is made in order to achieve the following six objectives:

1. To keep the American markets open for exports from Japan.
2. To smooth the way for additional purchases of key assets in the United States.
3. To blind criticism of Japan's adversarial trade practices.
4. To neutralize, or even better, to capture the political influence of the American firms that compete with Japan.
5. To influence United States trade policies toward Japan, Europe, and all other markets where Japan has significant economic interest.
6. To create an integrated American-Japanese economy that prevents the United States from confronting Japan economically and politically.

Choate, by describing Japan's tactics, is also showing how Japan has adhered to the major tenets of megamarketing. Japan is successfully implementing Kotler's concept of megamarketing by allocating to it significant funds, recognizing the importance of lobbyists to influence political leaders, adhering to long-term and continuous time frames, and using power when necessary to protect or advance its position.

American companies that have not recognized the importance of megamarketing and global strategies, like Silicon Valley's semiconductor industry, are shown by Choate to be unable to influence their "home" government to defeat Japanese positions which eventually leads to hurting themselves and the American economy.

Fernen Alden, in his 1987 article "Who Says You Can't Crack Japanese Markets?" supports Kotler's megamarketing concept and recommends finding partners who are politically connected to assist in breaking the barriers. He provides examples of American firms that have used their political influence to overcome foreign market barriers.

Silicon Valley firms need to successfully apply megamarketing concepts and therefore gain market access in order to satisfy, create or alter consumer demand. Silicon Valley firms will need to adjust to this new marketing paradigm.

DEVELOPING STRATEGIC MODELS FOR THE FUTURE

All businesses need some form of strategy to conduct their plans. Some develop formal strategies; in other cases, this is implied. Traditional strategic planning models evolved during the 1960s to "devise and implement strategies that would enhance the competitiveness of each business unit."[34] The traditional strategic models were in fact "strategic programming" processes, analytical in nature, requiring a calculating style of management according to Henry Mintzberg in his book *The Rise and Fall of Strategic Planning*.[35] He and other scholars argue that traditional strategic planning models are not relevant in today's technology-driven global competitive environment. They suggest replacing strategic planning with strategic thinking. Strategic planning is merely the "articulation and elaboration of strategies, or visions, that already exist," while strategic thinking is about synthesis, intuition, and creativity.[36]

The new strategic model derives its foundation from many unusual sources, including theories of evolution and skills of the craftsman. Bruce Henderson, in his article "The Origin of Strategy" bases its premise on Darwin's theory of natural selection and that lasting strategies, like the species, evolve and adapt to the changing environment. Those species that fail to adapt disappear. Similarly, in business "competitors perpetually crowd each other out. The fittest survive and prosper until they displace their competitors or outgrow their resources."[37] If a business is unable to create a unique advantage over its rivals, it will eventually cease to exist. The essence of his theme is that the new strategic model should constantly adapt to its competitive environment and consistently create new competitive advantages or face failure or decline.

In "Crafting Strategy," Henry Mintzberg describes new strategy formulation as an artform in which the artist "evokes traditional skill, dedication, perfection through the mastery of detail."[38] Strategic thinking can occur at any time, any place, and in any form, and it should not be restricted to formally timed planning processes. An artist has a vision of his end product and strives to achieve the result through detailed personal involvement. The future strategic model requires the dedicated involvement of the organization, a vision to produce the best outcome, and intimate knowledge of the details of how to make it work.

The three steps that are necessary for Silicon Valley firms to create a new strategic model are:

1. Developing a "Strategic Intent,"
2. Creating or identifying "core competencies," and
3. Challenging management to bridge the "stretch" between "intent" and "resources."[39]

The concept of "strategic intent" introduced by Gary Hamel and C.K. Prahalad in their 1989 article "Strategic Intent," provides a framework for business organizations centered on the strategies they must employ to gain global leadership. The concept was born from studying the success of firms that became dominant global corporations in less than twenty years, despite their starting with inferior technical ability and less manufacturing volume and resources than their competitors. These firms focused on resourcefulness rather than resources to guide their strategies. What the authors learned was that "Assessing the current tactical advantages of known competitors will not help you understand the resolution, stamina, and inventiveness of potential competitors."[40] But, to them, these firms "created an obsession with winning at all levels of the organization and then sustained that obsession over the 10-to-20-year quest for global leadership. We term this obsession 'strategic intent.'"[41] Developing strategic intent requires:

> "an active management process that includes: focusing the organization's intention on the essence of winning; motivating people by communicating the value of the target; leaving room for individual and team contributions; sustaining enthusiasm by providing new

> operational definitions as circumstances change; and using strategic intent consistently to guide resource allocations.[42]

Strategic intent is a commitment on the part of the organization as to what it wants to achieve thereby forcing the organization to be more creative in the use of its available resources. Strategic intent drives the resources it needs to innovate, rather than resources driving the strategic direction.

As Silicon Valley firms are challenged to create new advantages, the authors caution that "few competitive advantages are long lasting."[43] The firms must continuously strive to create new competitive advantages:

> Keeping score of existing advantages is not the same as building new advantages. The essence of strategy lies in creating tomorrow's competitive advantages faster than competitors mimic the ones you possess today. . . . an organization's capacity to improve existing skills and learn new ones is the most defensible competitive advantage of all.[44]

To win in global markets, the authors suggest four approaches to competitive innovation, the types of strategies that firms could use to gain competitive advantage over its rivals.

First is building layers of advantage that concentrate on winning one battle at a time over its rivals. Second is searching for loose bricks that uncovers different weakness in each competitor. Third is changing the terms of engagement which forces the competitor to meet you at your terms. And, fourth is competing through collaboration in which you join forces, sometimes even with your rivals, to beat a stronger opponent.

Strategic intent concentrates on creating new competitive advantages against different and potential competitors. The goal of the future strategist "is not to find a niche within the existing industry space but to create new space that is uniquely suited to the company's own strengths, space that is off the map."[45]

Once the organization creates an intent, it should develop or identify key core competencies. A core competency is a thorough mastery of some skills that a firm could utilize in order to enter various changing markets. This concept also has its roots in the theory of competitive advantage and has the underlying theme that global markets are rapidly changing and, to become a leader in the global marketplace, a company must not only synergize its interdependent worldwide resources, but it must also create "organizations capable of inventing new products, quickly entering markets, and dramatically shifting patterns of consumer choice in established markets," or "better yet, creating new products that customers need but have not yet even imagined."[46] If a company has such competency it can enter and change markets rapidly. Honda's competency in engines allows it to make cars, motorcycles, and lawnmowers: all using engines. NEC specializes in semiconductors, allowing it to be successful in computers and communications, both requiring semiconductors. IBM and AT&T both failed when they tried to enter the communications and computer fields respectively. Both approached them as business opportunities rather than having the core competency to respond to changing marketplace.

Core competencies are the "collective learning in the organization, especially how to coordinate diverse production skills and integrate multiple streams of technologies."[47] By developing core competencies, management attempts to inventory a set of skills and ensures that technicians and the marketers have a shared understanding of customer needs and of technological possibilities to meet the new demands of the global market.

By developing core competencies, successful firms add layers of competitive advantage by being able to supplement their cost and quality advantage with an "ability to invent new markets, create new products, and enhance them,"[48] and gaining access to a wide variety of markets. A case in point is Canon's competencies in optics and imaging allow it to create cameras and copiers, two very different markets, but with the same core competency.

To successfully implement the concept of core competencies, Prahalad and Hamel believe that the strategic business unit (SBU) structure of most U.S. diversified companies must be supplanted. The concepts of SBU and core competencies are compared in Figure 10.2.

FIGURE 10.2

TWO CONCEPTS OF THE CORPORATION:
SBU OR CORE COMPETENCIES

	SBU	Core Competency
Basis for competition	Competitiveness of today's products	Interfirm competition to build competencies
Corporate structure	Portfolio of businesses; related to product; market terms	Portfolio of competencies, core products, and businesses
Status of the business unit	Autonomy is sacrosanct; the SBU "owns" all resources other than cash	SBU is a potential reservoir of core competencies
Resource allocation	Discreet businesses are the unit of analysis; capital is allocated business by business	Businesses and competencies are the unit of analysis; top management allocates capital and talent
Value added of top management	Optimizing corporate returns through capital allocation trade-offs among businesses	Enunciating strategic architecture and building competencies to secure the future

The authors believe that by concentrating on end products produced by discreet business units, core competencies will be fragmented and will prevent the company from developing core products company-wide. The authors of the concept of core competencies believe "the inflexible SBU type organizations have contributed to the deskilling of some companies"[49] because in many instances the "single SBU is incapable of sustaining investment in core competence, and the only way it can remain competitive is to purchase key components from potential competitors."[50] The authors conclude that few companies with strong SBU orientation have built successful global distribution and brand positions.

The key lesson for existing or emerging Silicon Valley firms is to concentrate on developing core competencies that can be shared by the entire corporation rather that building fragmented and competing organizational structures.

To achieve competitive advantage managers need to be challenged. In an article "Strategy as Stretch and Leverage," published in 1993, authors Hamel and Prahalad suggest that corporations should create a stretch "a misfit between resources and aspirations," and challenge management to bridge that gap while at the same time forcing managers "to get the most out of the resources" available to them.[51] Their concept encourages the managers to be creative in inventing new ways to leverage the resources they have. In short:

> Strategy as stretch recognizes the essential paradox of competition: leadership cannot be planned for, but neither can it happen without a grand and well-considered aspiration.[52]

Technology will continue to dominate the future. As developing nations increase their standards of living, new markets will emerge. Global firms will have to muster whatever resource it takes to retain their competitive advantages. They must maintain their strategic intent to keep refining and reshaping their competencies. Through their core competencies they can create comparative advantage.

RETHINKING GOVERNMENT/INDUSTRY RELATIONSHIP

The industrial success of Japan and other Asian economies during the last twenty years owes much credit to their governments' economic and industrial policies. That issue has prompted questions regarding the United States government's responsibility in supporting industrial development. Many experts believe that the United States government support is necessary for Silicon Valley to be a viable competitor in the world microelectronics market. However, there seems to be little agreement as to what type of role the government should play.

The main issue here is that while the American business ideology generally forbids government involvement in promoting or supporting a specific firm or industry, most American firms that compete globally find themselves opposing their foreign rivals who are actively supported by their government. American ideology needs reevaluation. Robert Kuttner explains:

> The challenge in coming years is to reproduce the benefits that existed during the 30-year-long "American Century," but in a radically transformed institutional context. This will mean making several implicit policy goals explicit, many of which flatly contradict the economic philosophy that has guided U.S. policy for 40 years and that the government still seeks to export to the world.[53]

Silicon Valley initially benefited from the United States government's R&D investment and procurement policies. The only other time that the United States government has actively worked with Silicon Valley was to resolve semiconductor trade issues with Japan. This sporadic involvement is not conducive to a long-term healthy business environment.

To paraphrase Paul Krugman's competitive philosophy: it is firms that compete in global markets, only firms succeed or fail, not nations. Eventually, Silicon Valley firms will have to compete on their own merit in world markets.

The role, if any, of the United States government should be to assist Silicon Valley to develop, regain, and maintain comparative advantage. It can do so in two ways. Firstly, by providing a domestic infrastructure in which firms can develop their own competitive advantages. Key suggestions in support of that policy offered by local leaders are: investment in education, training, and development and availability of capital for startup companies.[54]

Secondly, influencing foreign governments, especially Japan, to offer equal access to American-made products in their markets.

Recently, the United States government announced a new policy to assist the American flat-panel display industry to compete against the Japanese who already dominate the market. *The Wall Street Journal* article stated:

> Without a substantial carrot from the government, many established companies say they won't make the private investments required to mount a challenge against Japan in advanced flat screens.[55]

However, this is not an example of a stable industrial policy but a reactive plan to assist a particular industry segment that has already lost its competitive advantage to the Japanese. According to the above article, "U.S. electronic companies, despite substantial government aid . . . still face long odds in their quest to become major manufacturers of flat display screens."[56]

In the future, Silicon Valley and the United States government should establish an industrial policy that (a) is stable over time, (b) is not reactive, and (c) promotes industry's competitiveness. However, Silicon Valley firms should not depend on the United States government to develop and maintain their competitive advantage; that is the responsibility of the firms themselves.

CAN SILICON VALLEY REINVENT ITSELF?

Definitely yes, but only if it adapts itself to the new global competitive realities. Not only will it need to innovate new technologies and products, but it will also need to innovate its management philosophies, its business practices, and organizational responsibilities. In essence, it will need to reinvent itself for the 21st century.

NOTES

1. Edward R. McCracken, "Reinventing the corporation," *San Jose Mercury News*, 3 April 1994, C1-C6.

2. *San Jose Mercury News*, 11 April 1994, 1D.

3. Michelle Levander, "More job nomads, fewer gold watches," *San Jose Mercury News*, 17 May 1992.

4. James J. Mitchell, "Summer slowdown? No way. Valley is working overtime," *San Jose Mercury News*, 29 August 1993, B1.

5. Ibid., B1.

6. Stratford Sherman, "The New Computer Revolution," *Fortune*, 14 June 1993, 56.

7. Peter Drucker, "The Coming of the New Organization," *Harvard Business Review* (January-February 1988), 45.

8. Peter Drucker, *Post-Capitalist Society* (New York: HarperBusiness, 1993), 8.

9. Kenichi Ohmae, *The Borderless World: Power and Strategy in the Interlinked Economy* (New York: HarperBusiness, 1990), 5.

10. *Business Week*, "The Technology Payoff," 14 June 1994, 57.

11. Michael T. Jacobs, *Short-Term America: The Causes and Cures of Our Business Myopia*," (Boston: Harvard Business School Press, 1991).

12. Charles Handy, *The Age of Unreason*, (Boston: Harvard Business School Press, 1989), 26.

13. Lester Thurow, "Revitalizing American Industry: Managing in a Competitive World Economy," *California Management Review* (Fall 1984), 19.

14. Homa Bahrami, "The Emerging Flexible Organization: Perspectives from Silicon Valley," *California Management Review* (Summer 1992), 48.

15. T. George Harris, "The Post-Capitalist Executive: An Interview with Peter F. Drucker," *Harvard Business Review* (May-June 1993), 115.

16. Ibid., 122.

17. Steven E. Prokesch, "Mastering Chaos at the High-Tech Frontier: An Interview with Silicon Graphic's Ed McCracken." *Harvard Business Review* (November-December 1993), 136.

18. Michael Hammer and James Champy, *Reengineering the Corporation* (New York: HarperBusiness, 1993), 2.
19. Michael E. Porter, "The Competitive Advantage of Nations," *Harvard Business Review* (March-April 1990), 74.
20. Ibid., 81.
21. Gary Hamel and C.K. Prahalad, "Strategy as Stretch and Leverage," *Harvard Business Review* (March-April 1993), 76.
22. Ibid., 76.
23. Ibid., 76.
24. Ibid., 77.
25. Arthur L. Money, "Real-world lessons for our schools," *San Jose Mercury News*, 17 April 1994, 1D.
26. George C. Lodge and Ezra F. Vogel, eds., *Ideology and National Competitiveness* (Boston: Harvard Business School Press, 1987), 23.
27. Ibid., 322.
28. Lodge, *Ideology and National Competitiveness*, 322.
29. Jacobs, *Short-Term America*, 9-10.
30. Gilbert Fuchsberg, "Business Schools Get Bad Grades," *The Wall Street Journal*, 6 June 1990, B1.
31. Philip Kotler, "Megamarketing," *Harvard Business Review* (March-April 1986), 118.
32. Ibid., 121.
33. Pat Choate, "Political Advantage: Japan's Campaign for America," *Harvard Business Review* (September-October 1990), 87-103.
34. Henry Mintzberg, "The Fall and Rise of Strategic Planning," *Harvard Business Review* (January-February 1994), 107.
35. Henry Mintzberg, *The Rise and Fall of Strategic Planning* (New York: The Free Press, 1994).
36. Mintzberg, *Harvard Business Review*, 107-8.
37. Bruce D. Henderson, "The Origin of Strategy," *Harvard Business Review* (November-December 1989), 140.
38. Henry Mintzberg, "Crafting Strategy," *Harvard Business Review* (July-August 1987), 66-9.

39. The terms "strategic intent," "core competencies," and "stretch" are used by Hamel and Prahalad in their articles and are later explained.

40. Gary Hamel and C.K. Prahalad, "Strategic Intent," *Harvard Business Review* (May-June 1989), 64.

41. Ibid., 64.

42. Ibid., 64.

43. Ibid., 69.

44. Ibid., 69.

45. Ibid., 73.

46. C.K. Prahalad and Gary Hamel, "The Core Competence of the Corporation," *Harvard Business Review* (May-June 1990), 80.

47. Ibid., 82.

48. Ibid., 83.

49. Ibid., 87.

50. Ibid., 87.

51. Hamel, *Strategy as Stretch and Leverage*, 78.

52. Ibid., 84.

53. Robert Kuttner, "How 'National Security' Hurts National Competitiveness," *Harvard Business School* (January-February 1991), 148.

54. James J. Mitchell, "These steps will make us more productive," *San Jose Mercury News*, 30 January 1994.

55. G. Pascal Zachary, "Road Toward Success at 'Flat Screen' is Full of Bumps," *The Wall Street Journal*, 29 April 1994, B4.

56. Ibid., B4.

Bibliography

BOOKS

Albrecht, Karl. *The Only Thing That Matters: Bringing the Power of the Customer into the Center of Your Business.* New York: HarperBusiness, 1992.

Batra, Ravi. *The Myth of Free Trade: A Plan for America's Economic Revival.* New York: Charles Scribner's Sons, 1993.

Bartlett, Christopher A. and Sumantra Ghoshal. *Managing Across Borders: The Transnational Solution.* Boston: Harvard Business School Press, 1989.

Burstein, Daniel. *Turning the Tables: A Machiavellian Strategy for Dealing with Japan.* New York: Simon and Schuster, 1993.

Cleveland, Harlan. *Birth of a New World: An Open Moment for International Leadership.* San Francisco: Jossey-Bass Publishers, 1993.

Cowhey, Peter F. and Jonathan D. Aronson. *Managing the World Economy: The Consequences of Corporate Alliances.* New York: Council on Foreign Relations Press, 1993.

Cringley, Robert X. *Accidental Empires: How The Boys of Silicon Valley Make Their Millions, Battle Foreign Competition, and Still Can't Get a Date.* New York: HarperCollins Publishers, 1992.

Davidow, William H. and Michael S. Malone. *The Virtual Corporation: Structuring and Revitalizing the Corporation for the 21st Century.* New York: HarperCollins Publishers, 1992.

Deken, Joseph. *The Electronic Cottage: Everyday Living with your Personal Computers in the 1980s.* New York: Bantam Books, 1981.

Dertouzous, Michael L., Richard K. Lester, and Solow M. Robert. *Made in America: Regaining the Productive Edge.* Cambridge, MIT Press, 1989.

de Tocqueville, Alexis. *Democracy in America.* New York: Penguin Press, 1956.

Dimancescu, Dan. *The Seamless Enterprise: Making Cross Functional Management Work.* New York: HarperCollins Publishers, 1992.

Drucker, Peter F. *The Practice of Management.* New York: Harper & Row, Publishers, 1954.

_____. *Innovation and Entrepreneurship*. New York: Harper Business, 1985.

_____. *The New Realities: In Government and Politics/In Economics and Business/In Society and World View*. New York: Harper & Row, 1989.

_____. *Managing for the Future: The 1990s and Beyond*. New York: Truman Talley Books/Dutton, 1992.

_____. *Post-Capitalist Society*. New York: Harper Business, 1993.

Durant, Will and Ariel Durant. *The Lessons of History*. New York: Simon & Schuster, 1968.

Evans, Christopher. *The Micro Millennium*. New York: Washington Square Press, 1979.

Forester, Tom. *High-Tech Society*. Boston: MIT Press, 1987.

Galbraith, John K. *The Affluent Society*. New York: The New American Library. 1959.

Handy, Charles. *The Age of Unreason*. Boston: Harvard Business School Press, 1989.

Hanson, Dirk. *The New Alchemists: Silicon Valley and the Micro-Electronics Revolution*. New York: Avon Books, 1982.

Hammer, Michael and James Champy. *Reengineering the Corporation: A Manifesto for Business Revolution*. New York: HarperBusiness, 1993.

Hampden-Turner, Charles and Alfons Trompenaars. *The Seven Cultures of Capitalism*. New York: Doubleday, 1993.

Hartley, Robert F. *Management Mistakes*. New York: John Wiley & Sons, 1986.

Jacobs, Michael T. *Short-Term America: The Causes and Cures of Our Business Myopia*. Boston: Harvard Business School Press, 1991.

Kennedy, Paul. *Preparing for the Twenty First Century*. New York: Random House, 1993.

Kleingartner, Archie and Carolyn S. Anderson, eds. *Human Resource Management in High Technology Firms*. Lexington: Lexington Books, 1987.

Krugman, Paul. *The Age of Diminished Expectations: U.S. Economic Policy in the 1990s*. Cambridge: The MIT Press, 1990.

_____. *Peddling Prosperity: Economic Sense and Nonsense in the Age of Diminished Expectations*. New York: W.W. Norton & Company, 1994.

Leebaert, Derek, ed. *Technology 2001: The Future of Computing and Communications*. Cambridge: MIT Press, 1991.

Lindert, Peter H. *International Economics*. Homewood: Richard D. Irwin, 1991.

Lodge, George C. *Perestroika for America: Restructuring Business-Government Relations for World Competitiveness*.Boston: Harvard Business School Press, 1990.

Lodge, George C. and Ezra F. Vogel, eds. *Ideology and National Competitiveness*. Boston: Harvard Press, 1987.

Maynard, Herman Bryant, Jr. and Susan E. Mehrtens. *The Fourth Wave: Business in the 21st Century*. San Francisco: Berrett-Koehler Publishers, 1993.

Machiavelli, Niccolo. *The Prince*. New York: Penguin Books, 1952.

McClellan, Stephen T. *The Coming Computer Industry Shakeout: Winners, Losers and Survivors*. John Wiley & Sons, 1984.

McCraw, Thomas K.,ed. *America versus Japan: A Comparative Study*. Boston: Harvard Business School Press, 1986.

Mintzberg, Henry. *The Rise and Fall of Strategic Planning*. NewYork: The Free Press, 1994.

Morita, Akia. *Made in Japan*. New York: Signet Books USA, 1986.

Naisbitt, John. *Megatrends: Ten New Directions Transforming Our Lives*. New York: Warner Books, 1982.

_____. *Global Paradox: The Bigger The World Economy, The More Powerful Its Smallest Players*. New York: William Morrow and Company, 1994.

Naisbitt, John and Patricia Aburdene. *Megatrends 2000:Ten New Directions for the 1990's*. New York: William Morrow and Company, 1990.

Ohmae, Kenichi. *Triad Power: The Coming Shape of Global Competition*. New York: The Free Press, 1985.

_____. *The Borderless World: Power and Strategy in the Interlinked Economy*. New York: Harper Business, 1990.

Ouchi, William G. *Theory Z: How American Business Can Meet the Japanese Challenge*. New York: Avon, 1981.

Peters, Thomas J. and Robert H. Waterman, Robert H. *In Search of Excellence: Lessons from America's Best-Run Companies*. New York: Harper & Row, 1982.

Peters, Tom and Nancy Austin. *A Passion for Excellence: The Leadership Difference*. New York: Random House, 1985.

Peters, Tom. *Thriving on Chaos: Handbook for a Management Revolution*. New York: Alfred A. Knopf, 1987.

Porter, Michael E., ed. *Competition in Global Industries*. Boston: Harvard Business School Press, 1986.

_____. *The Competitive Advantage of Nations*. New York: The Free Press, 1990.

_____. *Competitive Advantage: Creating and Sustaining Superior Performance*. New York: The Free Press, 1985.

Postman, Neil. *Technopoly: The Surrender of Culture to Technology*. New York: Alfred A. Knopf, 1992.

Reich, Robert. *The Work of Nations: Preparing Ourselves for 21st Century Capitalism*. New York: Alfred A. Knopf, 1991.

Riesman, David, Nathan Glazer, and Reuel Denney. *The Lonely Crowd: A Study of the Changing American Character*. New York: Doubleday Anchor Book, 1953.

Rogers, Everett M. and Judith K. Larsen. *Silicon Valley Fever: Growth of High-Technology Culture*. New York: Basic Books, 1984.

Root, Franklin R. *International Trade and Investment*. Cincinnati: South-Western Publishing Co., 1990.

Saxenian, Annalee. *Regional Advantage: Culture and Competition in Silicon Valley and Route 128*. Cambridge: Harvard University Press, 1994.

Sexton, Jean Deitz. *Silicon Valley: Inventing the Future*. Los Angeles: Windsor Publications, 1991.

Scott, Bruce R. and George C. Lodge, eds. *U.S. Competitiveness in the World Economy*. Boston, Massachusets: Harvard Press, 1985.

Scully, John. *Odyssey: Pepsi to Apple—A Journey of Adventure, Ideas, and the Future*. New York: Harper & Row, 1987.

Senge, Peter M. *The Fifth Discipline: The Art & Practice of The Learning Organization*. New York: Doubleday, 1990.

Smith, Adam. *The Wealth of Nations Books I-III*. New York: Penguin Books, 1986.

Tapscott, Don and Art Caston. *Paradigm Shift: The New Promise of Information Technology*. New York: McGraw Hill, 1993.

Toynbee, Arnold J. *A Study of History*. New York: Oxford University Press, 1946.

Thurow, Lester. *Head to Head: The Coming Economic Battle Among Japan, Europe, and America*. New York: William Morrow and Co., 1992.

Toffler, Alvin. *Power Shift: Knowledge, Wealth, and Violence at the Edge of the 21st Century*. New York: Bantam Books, 1990.

van Wolferen, Karel. *The Enigma of Japanese Power: People and Politics in a Stateless Nation*. New York: Alfred A. Knopf, 1989.

Wheelan, Thomas L. and David J. Hunger. *Strategic Management and Business Policy*. Reading: Addison-Wesley Publishing Company, 1989.

Whyte, William H., Jr. *The Organization Man*. New York: Simon and Schuster, 1956.

Wilson, Robert W., Peter K. Ashton, and Thomas P. Egan. *Innovation, Competition, and Government Policy in the Semiconductor Industry*. Lexington: Lexington Books, 1980.

GOVERNMENT/INDUSTRY PUBLICATIONS

American Electronics Association. *America's Future at Stake: Winning in the Global Marketplace*. 1989.

_____. *AEA Sacramento Caucus*. 7 February 1990.

Congress of the United States, Office of Technology Assessment. *Competing Economies: America, Europe, and the Pacific Rim*. Washington, D.C.: U.S. Government Printing Office, 1991.

Council on Research and Technology. *Coretech Policy Update: Section 861's Disincentive to Domestic R&D*. 1989.

Joint Venture: *Silicon Valley. An Economy At Risk: The Phase 1 Diagnostic Report*. August 1992.

SEMATECH. *Meeting America's Technology Challenge*. 1990.

Semiconductor Industry Association. *The Effect of Government Targeting on World Semiconductor Competition: A Case History of Japanese Industrial Strategy and Its Costs for America*. 1983.

_____. *Technology and Competitiveness*. 1992.

The United Nations. *Global Outlook 2000: An Economic, Social, and Environmental Perspective*. New York: 1990.

U.S. Department of Commerce. *The Competitive Status of the U.S. Electronics Sector from Materials to Systems*. Washington, D.C.: U.S. Government Printing Office, 1990.

U.S. Department of Commerce. *Statistical Abstract of the U.S.: The National Data Book 113th Edition. 1993*. Washington D.C.: U.S. Government Printing Office, 1993.

U.S. Department of Commerce, International Trade Administration.
*U.S. Industrial Outlook 1994: An Almanac of Industry,
Technology, and Services 35th Annual Edition.* January 1994.

JOURNALS

Adler, Paul. "New Technologies, New Skills." *California
Management Review* (1986): 9-28.

Adler, Paul S. and Kasra Ferdows. "The Chief Technology Officer."
California Management Review (Spring 1990): 55-62.

Amit, Raphael, Lawrence R. Glosten, and Eitan Muller. "Does
Venture Capital Foster the Most Promising Entrepreneurial
Firms?" *California Management Review* (Spring 1990): 102-11.

Bahrami, Homa. "The Emerging Flexible Organization: Perspectives
from Silicon Valley." *California Management Review* (Summer
1992): 33-52.

Bahrami, Homa and Stuart Evans. "Stratocracy in High-Technology
Firms." *California Management Review* (Fall 1987): 51-66.

_____. "Strategy Making in High-Technology Firms: The
Empiricist Mode." *California Management Review* (Winter 1989):
107-28.

Borrus, Michael. "Chip Wars: Can the U.S. Regain Its Advantage in
Microelectronics." *California Management Review* (Summer
1987): 64-79.

Bourgeois, L.J., III and Kathleen Eisenhardt. "Strategic Decision
Processes in Silicon Valley: The Anatomy of a 'Living Dead'."
California Management Review (Fall 1987): 143-59.

Choate, Pat. "Political Advantage: Japan's Campaign for America."
Harvard Business Review (September-October 1990): 87-103.

Cohen Stephen S., and John Zysman. "Why Manufacturing Matters:
The Myth of the Post-Industrial Economy." *California
Management Review* (1986): 9-26.

"Corporate Advantage-Identifying and Exploiting Resources."
Harvard Business Review (1991): 1-13.

Drucker, Peter F. "The Coming of the New Organization." *Harvard
Business Review* (January-February 1988): 45-53.

Florida, Richard and Martin Kenney. "Silicon Valley and Route 128
Won't Save Us." *California Management Review* (Fall 1990): 68-
88.

Galbraith, Craig S. "Transfering Core Manufacturing Technologies in High-Technology Firms." *California Management Review* (Summer 1990): 56-70.

"Global Semiconductor Industry-1987." *Harvard Business Review*, 1988: 1-21.

Gold, Bela. "Computerization in Domestic and International Manufacturing." *California Management Review* (Winter 1988): 129-143.

Grant, Robert M. "The Resource-Based Theory of Competitive Advantage: Implications for Strategic Formulation." *California Management Review* (Spring 1991): 114-35.

Greiner, Larry E. "Evolution and Revolution as Organizations Grow." *Harvard Business Review* (July-August 1972): 37-46.

Grove, Andrew. "Executive Forum: The Future of Silicon Valley." *California Management Review*, (Spring 1987): 154-60.

_____. "The Future of the Computer Industry." *California Management Review* (Fall 1990): 148-60.

Gupta, Ashok K., and David L. Wilemon. "Accelerating the Development of Technology-Based New Products." *California Management Review* (Winter 1990): 24-44.

Hamel, Gary and C.K. Prahalad. "Do You Really Have a Global Strategy." *Harvard Business Review* (July-August 1985): 139-48.

_____. "Strategic Intent." *Harvard Business Review* (May-June 1989): 63-76.

_____. "Strategy as Stretch and Leverage." *Harvard Business Review* (March-April 1993): 75-84.

Harrigan, Kathryn and Gaurav Dalmia. "Knowledge Workers: TheLast Bastion of Competitive Advantage." *Planning Review* (Nov/Dec 1991): 4-9.

Harris, T. George. "The Post-Capitalist Executive: An Interview with Peter F. Drucker." *Harvard Business Review* (May-June 1993): 115-122.

Hart, Jeffrey A. Laura Tyson. "Responding to the Challenge of HDTV." *California Management Review* (Summer 1989): 132-145.

Hayes, Robert H. and William J. Abernathy. "Managing Our Way to Economic Decline." *Harvard Business Review* (July-August 1980): 67-77.

Henderson, Bruce D. "The Origin of Strategy." *Harvard Business Review* (November-December 1989): 139-43.

Hout, Thomas, Michael E. Porter, and Eileen Rudden. "How Global
    Companies Win Out." *Harvard Business Review* (September-
    October 1982): 98-108.

"Intel Corporation 1988." *Harvard Business Review* (1989): 1-12.

Kotler, Philip. "Megamarketing." *Harvard Business Review* (March-
    April 1986): 117-24.

Krugman, Paul. "Competitiveness: A Dangerous Obsession." *Foreign
    Affairs* (March/April 1994): 28-44.

Kuttner, Robert. "How 'National Security' Hurts National
    Competitiveness." *Harvard Business Review* (January-February
    1991): 140-9.

Levitt, Theodore. "Marketing Myopia." *Harvard Business Review*
    (1960): 1-15.

_____. "The Globalization of Markets." *Harvard Business Review*
    (May-June 1983): 92-102.

"Loss of U.S. Dominance in DRAMs: A Case History-1976-84."
    Harvard Business Review (1989): 1-18.

Miles, Raymond E. "Adapting to Technology and Competition: A
    New Industrial Relations System for the 21st Century." *California
    Management Review* (Winter 1988): 9-28.

Mintzberg, Henry. "Crafting Strategy." *Harvard Business Review*
    (July-August 1987): 66-75.

_____. "The Fall and Rise of Strategic Planning." *Harvard
    Business Review* (January-February 1994): 107-14.

Mowery, David C. and Nathan Rosenberg. "New Developments in
    U.S. Technology Policy: Implications for Competitiveness and
    International Trade Policy." *California Management Review* (Fall
    1989): 107-24.

Nelson, Richard. "Recent Writing on Competitiveness: Boxing the
    Compass." *California Management Review* (Winter 1992): 127-
    37.

"National Semiconductor and SEMATECH." *Harvard Business
    Review* (1992): 1-19.

"Note on Comparative Advantage." *Harvard Business Review* (1986):
    1-8.

"Note on Global Technology Flows." *Harvard Business Review*
    (1989): 1-8.

"Note on Microcomputers: Overview of PCs and Workstations."
    Harvard Business Review (1989): 1-14.

"Note on Sources of Comparative Advantage." *Harvard Business Review* (1986): 1-7.

Ohe, Takeru, Shuji Honjo, Mark Oliva, and Ian MacMillan. "Entrepreneurs in Japan and Silicon Valley: A Study of Perceived Differences." *Journal of Business Venturing* (March 1991): 135-44.

Pavitt, Keith. "What We Know about the Strategic Management of Technology." *California Management Review* (Spring 1990): 17-26.

Porter, Michael E. "From Competitive Advantage to Corporate Strategy." *Harvard Business Review* (May-June 1987): 43-59.

_____. "The Competitive Advantage of Nations." *Harvard Business Review* (March-April 1990): 73-93.

Prahalad, C.K. and Gary Hamel. "The Core Competence of the Corporation." *Harvard Business Review* (May-June 1990): 79-91.

Prokesch, Steven E. "Mastering Chaos at the High-Tech Frontier: An Interview with Silicon Graphics's Ed McCracken," *Harvard Business Review* (November-December 1993): 135-44.

Saxenian, AnnaLee. "Regional Networks and the Resurgence of Silicon Valley." *California Management Review*, (Fall 1990): 89-111.

"Sematech: Innovation for America's Future." *Harvard Business Review* (1988): 1-31.

"Semiconductor Industry Association and the Trade Dispute with Japan" *Harvard Business Review* (1987): 1-17.

Thomas, Tom E. "Has Business 'Captured' the California Initiative Agenda?" *California Management Review* (Fall 1990): 131-47.

Thurow, Lester. "Revitalizing American Industry: Managing in a Competitive World Economy." *California Management Review* (Fall 1984): 9-41.

Tyebjee, Tyzoon T. "A Typology of Joint Ventures: Japanese Strategies in the United States. "*California Management Review* (Fall 1989): 75-86.

Yoffie, David B. "How An Industry Builds Political Advantage: Silicon Valley goes to Capitol Hill." *Harvard Business Review* (May-June 1988): 82-9.

MAGAZINE ARTICLES

"A Survey of the Computer Industry." *The Economist* (27 February 1993): 1-18.

Bergstrom, Robin P. "Travail in Silicon Valley." *Production* (September 1992): 36-43.

Bovard, James. "Toxic Dumping." *The New Republic* (9 December 1991): 18.

Brandt, Richard, Jonathan B. Levine, Robert D. Hof, John Carey, and Otis Port. "The Future of Silicon Valley." *Business Week* (5 February 1990): 54-60.

"Business: How Grey is My Valley." *The Economist* (23 March 1991): 71-2.

Carey, John. "One Stepper Forward for Sematech." *Business Week* (8 June 1992): 110-2.

"Deconstructing The Computer Industry." *Business Week* (23 November 1992): 90-100.

"Did Commerce Pull the Plug on Flat-Screen Makers?" *Business Week* (5 July 1993): 32.

"Economic miracle or myth?" *The Economist* (2 October 1993): 41.

Fallows, James. "Containing Japan." *The Atlantic Monthly* (May 1989): 40-54.

_____. "Getting Along With Japan." *The Atlantic Monthly* (December 1989): 53-64.

_____. "Looking At The Sun." *The Atlantic Monthly* (November 1993): 69-100.

_____. "How the World Works." *The Atlantic Monthly* (December 1993): 60-102.

_____. "What is an Economy For?" *The Atlantic Monthly* (January 1994): 76-92.

Krugman, Paul. "Competitiveness: Does it Matter?" *Fortune* (7 March 1994): 109-15.

Mann, Charles. "The Man With All The Answers." *The Atlantic Monthly* (January 1990): 45-62.

"Modern Wonders: The age of the thing." *The Economist* (25 December 1993-7 January 1994): 47-48.

Morita, Akio. "Toward a New World Economic Order." *The Atlantic Monthly* (June 1993): 88-98.

Morris, Charles R. "It's not the economy, stupid." *The Atlantic Monthly* (July 1993): 49-62.

Peter Drucker's 1990s: The futures that have already happened." *The Economist* (21 October 1989): 19-20.

Peterson, Peter G.. "The Morning After." *The Atlantic Monthly* (October 1987): 43-69.

Pouschine, Tatiana. "Technology is slamming right into the regulatory machinery." *Forbes* (16 April 1990).

Reich, Robert B. "The REAL Economy." *The Atlantic Monthly* (February 1991): 35-52.

Sherman, Stratford. "The New Computer Revolution." *Fortune* (14 June 1993): 56-81.

"Silicon Valley." *Business Week* (Enterprise 1993): 169-83.

"The Survey of America." *The Economist* (26 October 1991): 1-26.

"The Technology Payoff." *Business Week* (14 June 1993): 57-79.

"What's Wrong?: Why the Industrialized Nations are Stalled." *Business Week* (2 August 1993): 54-60.

"Why Japan Can Still Say No." *Business Week* (5 July 1993): 70-74.

Wise, Ray. "Aggressive Japanese Venture Capital Worries Silicon Valley." *Electronic Business* (11 June 1990): 57-58.

Wrubel, Robert. "Silicon Valley Squirms." *Financial World* (20 March 1990): 58-61.

Young, Lewis H. "Let's Talk Trade." *Electronic Business* (August 1993): 28-36.

NEWSPAPER ARTICLES

Burke, Gary. "Vision of a Valley that works." *San Jose Mercury News* (22 March 1994).

Burke, William M. "Dead Economist Getting His Due." *San Francisco Chronicle* (28 February 1994): B3.

Clark, Don. "Jobs Coming and Going in Silicon Valley." *San Francisco Chronicle* (7 July 1993): E1 and E3.

Collins, James. "Silicon Valley's big myth: Track to business success isn't fast." *San Jose Mercury News* (28 June 1992): 1C and 8C.

Davis, Bob and G. Pascal Zachary. "Electronic Firms Get Push From Clinton to Join Industrial Policy Initiative in Flat-Panel Displays." *The Wall Street Journal* (28 April 1994): A16.

Eckhouse, John. "Carla Hills Rattles Chip Firms." *San Francisco Chronicle* (1 February 1992): B1 and B3.

Fisher, Lawrence M. "7 Makers Plan Chip Venture: U.S. Memories Set to Make D-RAM's." *The New York Times* (22 June 1989).

Fuchsberg, Gilbert. "Business Schools Get Bad Grades." *The Wall Street Journal* (6 June 1990).

Gomes, Lee. "How PC changed the face of valley." *San Jose Mercury News* (16 April 1994): 11D.

_____. "White House promises another $300 million for flat panel." *San Jose Mercury News* (29 April 1994): 1E and 2E.

Hamilton, David P. "U.S., Japan Focusing On Electronic Gear." *The Wall Street Journal* (12 July 1993).

Langberg, Mike. "Antitrust objections called unlikely." *San Jose Mercury News* (22 June 1989).

Levander, Michelle. "More job nomads, fewer gold watches." *San Jose Mercury News* (17 May 1992): 1A and 20A.

_____. "Electronics job loss high." *San Jose Mercury News* (20 April 1994): 9D and 15D.

Kaufman, Steve. "Study questions origin of Silicon Valley slump." *San Jose Mercury News* (28 June 1992): 1E and 6E.

Krugman, Paul. "Competitiveness, a Dangerous Obsession." *The Wall Street Journal* (28 February 1994).

Lachica, Eduardo. "U.S. Removes Licensing Rules on Export of High-Tech Products." *The Wall Street Journal* (13 July 1989).

McCracken, Edward R. "Reinventing the corporation: Silicon Valley has learned to deal with rapid change." *San Jose Mercury News* (3 April 1994): C5-C6.

Malone, Michael S. "A capital offense: Class comes to the valley." *San Jose Mercury News* (13 May 1990): 1C and 5C.

Marshall, Jonathan, "Reinventing the Workforce: A talk with Labor Secretary Reich." *San Francisco Chronicle* (22 February 1994): D1 and D5.

_____. "Trade Barriers Blamed on U.S." *San Francisco Chronicle* (February 1994): E1 and E2.

Mitchell, James J. "Valley business profits big from Stanford's role." *San Jose Mercury News* (29 June 1993).

_____. "Summer slowdown? No way. Valley is working overtime." *San Jose Mercury News* (29 August 1993).

_____. "Alliances make individualistic firms stronger." *San Jose Mercury News* (17 October 1993).

_____. "How Silicon Valley can keep from drifting in a sea of change." *San Jose Mercury News* (2 January 1994): 1E and 8E.

_____. "These steps will make us more competitive." *San Jose Mercury News* (30 January 1994).

Money, Arthur L. "Real-world lessons for our schools." *San Jose Mercury News* (17 April 1994): 1D and 3D.

Passell, Peter. "Economic Scene: U.S. Memories: Who is the Loser?" *The New York Times* (24 January 1990).

Rankin, Robert A. and Tom Schmitz. "Government should bolster firms to meet competitors, report says." *San Jose Mercury News* (14 November 1991): 1A.

Rice, Valerie. "Sematech unveils 5-year plan." *San Jose Mercury News* (1991).

_____. "Milpitas firm quits Sematech venture." *San Jose Mercury News* (December 1991): 1A and 8A.

Schmitz, Tom and Kristin Huckshorn. "Export changes to boost valley." *San Jose Mercury News* (30 September 1993): 1A.

Schrage, Michael. "Competitiveness is a dead end for U.S., MIT economist says." *San Jose Mercury News* (14 March 1994).

Siegel, Lenny. "Valley Future: Social critic finds reason for optimism." *San Jose Mercury News* (3 January 1993): 1C and 8C.

Siegel, Lenny. "Target real enemy of trade." *San Jose Mercury News* (1990).

Siegman, Ken. "Silicon Valley Copes With Hard Times." *San Francisco Chronicle* (20 July 1993): D1 and D2.

_____. "Courtroom Chip War Resumes: It's AMD vs. Intel in copyright case." *San Francisco Chronicle* (November 1993): B1 and B6.

_____. "Computer Chips Take Center Stage in Daily Life." *San Francisco Chronicle* (20 December 1993): B1and B3.

_____. "U.S. Takes Back Lead In Chips." *San Francisco Chronicle* (December 1993): D1 and D4.

_____. "An American Tale of Semi-Success." *San Francisco Chronicle* (20 December 1994): B1 and B6.

"Silicon Valley 150: It's a Whole, New Universe." *San Jose Mercury News* (12 April 1993): 1E-10E.

"Silicon Valley 150: Riding High." *San Jose Mercury News* (11 April 1994): 1D-12D.

Smith, Rebecca. "U.S. chip firms bemoan dip in Japanese market share." *San Jose Mercury News* (23 September 1993).

_____. "U.S. regains chip lead." *San Jose Mercury News* (15 December 1993): 1F and 2F.

_____. "AMD victory over Intel to swell PC chip supply." *San Jose Mercury News* (11 March 1994): 1A and 20A.

Taylor, Timothy. "Valley demise is greatly exaggerated." *San Jose Mercury News* (1993).

Tyson, Laura D. "Japan's Trade Surplus Matters." *The Wall Street Journal* (1 March 1994).

Wolf, Ron. "Valley firms defy year of bad news." *San Jose Mercury News* (11 April 1993): 1A.

Zachary, G. Pascal. "Road Toward Success at 'Flat Screen' is Full of Bumps." *The Wall Street Journal* (29 April 1994): B4.

Zielenziger, Michael and Steve Kaufman. "A Prescription for Silicon Valley's Trade Ills." *San Jose Mercury News* (20 July 1993): 1E and 7E.

Index